HEY WOMEN !

BE LIMITLESS

DR. MUKTA GOYAL SANJAY GOYAL

Contents

Preface   *v*

1. Women's Empowerment And Economic Development In India   1

2. Women's Empowerment Through Education   9

3. Women Education In Modern Society   16

4. Education Status Of Tribal Women In India   23

5. The Fight Against Triple Talaq   28

6. Government Initiatives For Women's Empowerment   41

7. Post-pandemic Impact On Indian Working Women   49

8. Women Entrepreneurship In India   57

9. Teacher As A Leader   61

10. Empowering Women In Times Of Bloodshed   69

References   77

Preface

Empowerment of women means raising women as more aware individuals, who are economically productive and independent and are able to make their own decisions related to education and their own health. The main objective of women's empowerment is to ascertain gender equality. Thus, making sure that women workers are provided with equal facilities in terms of their overall welfare and safety at workplaces. Women empowerment has been an ever-rising global topic for ages now. Women's economic empowerment is a prerequisite for sustainable development and pro-poor growth. Achieving women's economic empowerment requires sound public policies, a holistic approach and long-term commitment and gender-specific perspectives must be integrated at the design stage of policy and programming. Women must have more equitable access to assets and services; Infrastructure programmes should be designed to benefit the poor, both men and women, and employment opportunities must be improved while increasing recognition of women's vast unpaid work. Innovative approaches and partnerships include increased dialogue among development actors, improved coordination amongst donors and support for women organising at the national and global levels. This book focuses on the importance of women's empowerment, women's education, and various government initiative for women's empowerment.

Without gender equality and empowerment, the country could not be just, and social change wouldn't occur. Therefore, scholars agree that women's empowerment plays a huge role in development and is one of the significant contributions to development.

Dr Mukta Goyal
Sanjay Goyal

CHAPTER ONE

Women's Empowerment and Economic Development in India

Introduction

Women's liberation means the social, physical, political and legal influence of women to be strengthened and improved so that women have equality of rights. Empowerment of women allows women to monitor, take advantage of and maintain their own resource, money, jobs, time, and risks and improve their economic situation and well-being. Many of the challenges found in societal expectations are women's rights and justice. There are many women who face these stresses, while most are used to being viewed differently than men. Enabling women to engage fully in economic life in all fields is critical to developing stronger economies, meeting globally agreed targets of growth and resilience and improving women, men, families and societies' quality of life. In developed countries, promoting women is a crucial problem. While women are an integral part of every community, their role in decision-making is not important by their active contribution in economic activities. Women's empowerment and economic growth are linked, with development alone playing a major role in mitigating gender disparity on the one hand, while women will benefit from development on the other.

"You can tell the condition of nation by looking the status of the women"
– Pt. Jawaharlal Nehru

The role of Indian women in their homes and their jobs took on a multifaceted dimension during the period of globalisation. The contribution of women is increasingly rising in India, as one of the most rapidly developing economies. Most Indian women perform "productive work" only under economic pressure and in general. Most women are seen working in agricultural and unorganised operations, and women have a strong employment in some occupations, such as part-time assistants in homes, houses, tanneries, match boxes etc. The growing role of women has been a key engine of economic development in the last century. This empowerment takes several forms: expanded involvement in female employment, decreased sexism, and pay differentials that encourage greater effort and better promotion practises in leadership and leadership positions for talented female workers. Women's empowerment needs to begin with engagement in diverse fields of life.In this sense, schooling is a big determinant. Women must be taught to understand their rights and freedoms in a modern world in order to gain empowerment. It is education in them that will raise consciousness of their social standing, inequality and difference. Moreover, economic autonomy is an important element in empowering women.

India is the largest democracy in the world with 1,186,200,000 inhabitants and almost half women. So how the condition of women affects the growth of India. The Nobel Prize winner in the field of economics, Amartya Sen, goes beyond fundamental ideas on the industrial use of consumer goods to even understand the use of commodities by the consumer. Sen clearly suggests that it is how any one of us uses the things that matter and should use them; a personalise approach. Your utility varies from that of a bread loaf. It varies due, among other factors, to its body size, activity level and fitness. Only a basic product such as bread can differ from person to person. Sen considers this feature. Capacity is a product feeling evoking, for example, a bike but a bicycle usefulness. For example, Sen accepts actual sales, but reverses the revenue and states that the product must be converted into health and education. The United Nations Human Development Index (HDI) has influenced Sen's vision (Todaro and Smith, 2006).

The empowerment of women in the economy refers to women's right to monitor and take advantage of wealth, properties, income and time, and to mitigate risk, and improve their economic and welfare status. Empowering women and achieving gender equality is critical to ensuring equitable country growth in our society. Sustainable development, including women's empowerment, is acceptable to environmental security, social and economic progress. Sustainable development, including women's empowerment, will not be accomplished without equity. The equal involvement of both men and women is generally considered to be crucial for progress. Sustainable development would not benefit only from the acknowledgment of men's participation. Empowerment should provide more options for women to select themselves in the sense of women and growth. The country will not be equitable and social reform wouldn't take place without gender equality and empowerment. Economic capability strengthens women's organisations, access to governmental formal services, domestic mobility, economic freedom and purchasing power. Policymakers are recommended to promote career experience to help organised market entry. One suggestion is to provide women with more formal education resources to improve their bargaining power at home. It would make it possible for women to find a position in the industry and thus have more access to better pay outside the building.

Strengthening women's access to land and property rights is another tool used to motivate women economically. This will allow them to further acquire money, resources, and negotiation leverage to deal with gender inequality. The right to land gives women a kind of bargain-making authority which they usually will not have; in its turn, women get more opportunities for economic freedom and structured financial institutions. Sometimes, women in the developing and underdeveloped world are constitutionally restricted from their own countries by gender alone.

Empowerment can be seen as having a social atmosphere in which individual or group actions and options for social change can be created. Empowerment increases latent potential through the accumulation of information, power and experience (Hashemi Schuler and Riley, 1996). Empowerment is the mechanism by which persons are empowered to think, act and regulate An independent way. An independent way. It's the way you can influence the fate of yourself and the life circumstances. There are still those elements in society who in every society, state and country have been stripped of their basic rights, but they are unaware of their rights. Women would be at the top of this list if we mentioned those elements of culture. Indeed, women play a leading role in all cultures. While everybody knows this, no one is willing to embrace it. Consequently, the significance of women in today's culture has declined. The need for women to be empowered became felt as a result of this growing propensity to underestimate women to be secondary to society and to strip women of their fundamental rights. Strong debates and attention around the world have been focused on promoting women. Nowadays, we have the advantages of being citizens of a free nation but we still need to understand if any resident of our world, in the true sense of the word, is really free or free. Discrimination and inequality amongst men and women remain a long-standing problem in the planet. So the quest for equality between women and men is a common practise. In matters of education, work, heritage, marriage and politics etc., women should be equal to men. Thus, empowerment means a psychological sense of personal control or influence and a concern with actual social influence, political power and legal rights. It is a multi-level construct referring to individuals, organizations and community. It is an international, ongoing process centred in the local community, involving mutual respect, critical reflection, caring and group participation, through which people lacking an equal share of valued resources gain greater access to the control over this resources.

Education in India

Elementary universal education for children aged between 6 and 14 years has been provided in India since 1960. Primary and high schools which the government owns are open, but are not considered to provide high-level education. In standards, as well as in rural and urban standards, there are great geographical variations. The state of Kerala for example, where 90% of the population are educated and 39% in the state of Bihar. Female and male disparity can also be found in school. For adults, literacy is 75%, and for women it is 64%. These above-mentioned gaps cause schooling instead of reducing discrimination. They move from their hometown as women marry. This makes daughter's parents unlike their sons' long lasting stimulus to invest in education. Girls are usually assigned to college instead. When men get married, they sit and care for their parents as they get older. This provides parents the opportunity to invest in the schooling of their son, which is sometimes compensated by jobs of the daughter (Todaro and Smith, 2006).

• Observational evidence has found that uneducated women impede economic progress and increase social inequality. Women's education has a higher rate of return in most developed countries than men's.

• Trained moms build greater school and healthy opportunities for children than improved salaries. If women are not qualified, it produces a bad loop, through the children of untrained women and the future of children, and the future of the world.

• India spends more in higher education, not primary or secondary education which may help a greater mass of people.

• Teachers are another concern in India. In a 1999 survey by the Basic Education Public Study (PROBE), they did so.It was only served by half of the students.

Secondary education is particularly important for breaking down the poverty heritage of India from one generation to the next. Recent analysis indicates that secondary education is particularly important. Many of the reasons for this is that its median privately held returns on additional education are the highest.

Educational equality

Another area in which women's equality has shown a major improvement as a result of adult literacy programs is the area of enrolment of boys and girls in schools. As a result of higher participation of women in literacy campaigns, the gender gap in literacy levels is gradually getting reduced. Even more significant is the fact that disparity in enrolment of boys and girls in neo-literate households is much lowered compared to the non-literate householders. The world has achieved equality in primary education between girls and boys. But few countries have achieved that target at all levels of education. The political participation of women keeps increasing. In January 2014, in 46 countries more than 30% of members of parliament in at least one chamber were women. In many countries, gender in equality persists and women continue to face discrimination in access to education, work and economic assets, and participation in government.

Importance of Women participation

The area of enrolment of boys and girls in schools has also shown substantial changes as a result of adult education programmes. The gender disparity in literacy rate is steadily being narrowed as a result of the expanded participation of women in literacy campaigns. Perhaps more critical than non-literate households, the fact that the difference in the registration of girls or boys in obliterate households is significantly diminished. Fair primary education for girls and boys has been achieved in the country. However, few countries at all levels of education have accomplished that goal. Women's political presence continues to expand. About 30 percent of parliamentarians in at least one House were women in 46 countries in January 2014. Sex in feminism exists in many countries and women are also discriminated against when it comes to access to schooling, jobs and economic assets and government engagement. Participation by women can be used by both an organisation to assist them and the lawmakers as a monitoring mechanism. Participation may be overt or indirect, formal or informal; in nature it could be democratic, social or administrative. Women can take several forms of participation in Panchayat Raj institutions. It refers to any of the initiatives showing a women's engagement and management of the strategies and services targeted at the growth target groups. It refers to engage in policy design and programme preparation, policy execution and assessment. Since pre-independence, Indian women have been active in politics. They were both volunteers and participants of the independence struggle. As regards freedom, the dignity granted to women by law under Article 15 of the Indian Constitution. Although all people have equal rights under the Indian constitution, women continue to be marginally represented in the Indian arena. The reality is that the centre and state loses influence in women's hands. It is unfortunate that nearly half the Indian population accounts for just 10% of the locomotive. There are 21 women in the present Rajya Sabha out of a total of 233 MPs, which is just 9% less than that in the locomotive sabha. Male control of Parliament, administration, the courts, the military, and police at social level all point to gender disparity, despite the fact that women's leadership is frequently argued in favour of a more cooperative and less conflict-prone society. The lack of political and economic influence contributes to the subdural and inequalities of women. India was unable to attain universal values like fairness, equity and social justice despite having its own constitution. Also seeing a woman Prime Minister after just a few years has not changed the status of women. The representation of women in politics worldwide was first put on board in the mid-1970s, when the UN proclaimed 1975 as the International Year of Women. The United Nations' decade for women was accompanied by "Equality, Development and Peace" between1976 and1985. Women's role in politics remains quite uneven in India today, but some changes were made by the seventy-third and seventy-fourth constitutional amendments, which improved women's political standing through opportunities for women to take decisions. The 73rd and 74th amendments (1993) on India's constitution have provided for the quota, laying a solid basis for their inclusion in decision-making in local bodies of panchayats and municipalities for women.

Female Labour Force Participation

The school system and the population connect. In India, demand for professional and semi-qualified jobs is growing in rural, urban and international regions (Secondary education in India). The informal sector is under- or under-educated, uses labour-intensive rather than capital-intensive technologies, is unqualified and has no convenient access to finance capital. (Smith and Todaro, 2006). Nine of ten women in India work in the informal sector unless we take women into account in agriculture. This homework simplifies the combining of work and family for women and encourages the whole family, including girls, to participate (Lim, 2003). The Self Employed Women's Association (SEWA) syndicate registered in 1972 organises females in India working in the informal sector. This organisation is a forum to achieve full employment and social stability for women in the informal sector. The company offers women grants, children's services, dental care and insurance. This way has expanded around the globe, such as the South African Self-employed Women's Union (sewa.org)

• In India, the beedis industry hires 5 million employees, of which 90% are women who work for US$ 1/day, whether they roll 1000 beds the same day. This work is normally home-based, which encourages women's engagement in the work (Lim, 2003).

The feminization of labour has grown in two ways: the rise of paying jobs by women and, through the informal sector, for example the increase in demand for a more mobile workforce between men and women. However, Boser up had right to say that it would be for the unqualified low-wage workers if they were employed in the new industry. The rise in salaries did not diminish women's unpaid jobs, for example, taking care of other members of the family. Unpaid employment adversely impacts the wage work of women and can also lead to girls being taken from school at home.

Conclusion

Women play an important role in increasingly developing a country. They are vital possession of a vibrant humanity that is crucial for national improvement, and thus if we are to see a promising future for women in our world, emancipation means moving from a vulnerable place to exercise power to provide them with education. Women's education is the most important instrument for shifting society's position. Training also decreases inequality and works in order to improve their family status.

The Indian government should introduce policies in favour of childcare facilities that can have an effect on women who want to become jobs. Today, 25 families, mainly women, look after them, have solved this situation. But childcare facilities will encourage these women relatives to join the workforce as well. Another concept which also relates to the treatment of the aged, which now exists, is solved by the woman family members, most of whom are infants. SEWA, once again, for example, supports its participants with child care. But the government also has to do more, and these facilities will give people a chance to work, because women in these careers are mostly involved.

Women play a significant role in India's economy and their efforts must be thoroughly accepted. Women ought to be encouraged and strengthened in order to improve their efficiency.

Women's Empowerment Through Education

Introduction:

Women's empowerment is the most conversational topic today. Women are given more power to decide their lives and career opportunities to understand their full potential. In order to combat gender-based discrimination, they must swim against a system where it requires more power. Such power that comes during the enable process, that comes from education. "As the World Conference on Development and Development states: "Education is one of the most important ways to empower women with the knowledge, skills and confidence needed to participate fully in the development process". There is no doubt that during that time the status of women has improved economically, socially and politically. They were striving to achieve gender equality in terms of job opportunities and to improve existing legislation. Establishing women's identity is a key activity in empowering women. Nowadays a variety of subjects and discussions are considered female identity where the name of Malala Yousafzai receives the most special attention. Malala Yousafzai has emerged as the strongest woman in the modern world by challenging people who threatened her with death for voicing the basic educational rights of women. As well as an example for many children in all parts of the World. Currently Indian women are able to perform as many social functions as men. They represent half of the population and play an essential role in all aspects of life. Many Indian women occupy various prestigious positions in diverse offices. The Government of India viewed 2001 as a year of empowerment of women. As part of the celebration of International Women's Day, Rajyasabha passed the Women's Reservation Bill which guaranteed the 33% reservation of women in parliament and state legislatures. The Bill was introduced in

March 2010. After giving the reservation the women continue to suffer because of the culture and traditions that exist.

There is no denying that the world holds some form of open discrimination against men and women, even though there is every feminist talking about gender equality. Education plays a vital role in building and nurturing the minds of the next generation toward gender equality. Ironically, however, the modern education system, especially in the rural areas of the country, still gender biased in different ways. There are many challenges faced by girls in schools due to gender bias in society, which has led them to take on a marginal role instead of raising them as independent women. Educators need to understand the importance of impartial education, by treating girls and boys equally in the education sector to help eradicate all forms of gender bias in our society. In the present case, what happens most is that when a girl enters school life, is seen as a player, she is actually better than most boys, and is almost equal to them in various aspects of education. But over time, upon graduation, their career growth and success are lagging behind. This is because of the way boys and girls are raised as children and how they are influenced by sexiest stereotypes and social myths. This is clearly reflected in the men's and women's education levels in India, which were found to be 82.14% for men and 65.46% for women according to the 2011 Census.

Women play a vital role in the development of the family, community and country. In order to build democracy to be successful in the country, education for women is needed along with men. Educated women are a real source of happiness in the family. Education is one of the landmarks of women's empowerment because it enables them to face their challenges, traditional roles and change their way of life (Bhat, 2015). The literacy rate for women in India is lower than from men. Compared to boys few girls are enrolled in schools and many drop out. "Educate the Girl, Empower the Nation." Women play a vital role in the development of the nation. In this century the world economy depends not only on men but also on women. To improve the role of women in society the government focused on their education and increased employment opportunities. In these circumstances, we need the continued development of gender equality, literacy and the empowerment of women in all parts of India. As a result, the Government of India has introduced a number of programs and programs for inclusion in the development agenda. These practices have brought about significant changes in the social and economic conditions of women. After India gained independence, the participation of nationalistic women was widely accepted. When the Constitution of India was drafted, it gave equal rights to women, regarding them as legitimate citizens of the country and as equals for men with freedom and opportunity. Free and compulsory education for children between the ages of 6 and 14 is a fundamental right of Indian citizens under the Indian Constitution under 86th Amendment. Although the Indian government has taken steps such as "Sarva Shiksha Abhiyan" (the main purpose of this program is to provide primary education, especially for girls from India, in poor rural areas). Despite these activities there are many barriers to women.

Women empowerment through education

Considering all women in society, the percentage of educated women is much lower than that of men. The importance of women's education is briefly summarized.

- Education helps women to come forward with confidence in the future and will be able to eradicate gender inequality and injustice.
- As long as women go back, they will not be able to enjoy the safety and security of life. But through education women can find financial opportunities, job opportunities and a safe working environment.
- Education helps women to live a dignified life as a person in society and also helps to understand their rights in society. However they are able to find a quick and easy legal battle against the major forms of violence against women such as rape, dowry, forced prostitution, child marriage, and female feticide and so on.
- Education helps women understand the importance of health and fitness of the body and helps them to lead healthier lives.
- Education helps women to prove to be more successful in the field of health. Inspite getting equal chances she could be successful doctors, engineers, nurses, an airline pilot, or even a career. If girls and women do not have the right to education, our society will not have social and economic development.

'Gandhi emphasized the need for compulsory education for girls, remembering that it was an important way to' empower women to secure their natural rights, use them wisely and work for their own development and to free themselves from male domination. According to Gandhi, "An uneducated person is no different from an animal. He emphasized the need for education that would support women to think for themselves. She pointed out that today very few women are involved in politics and most of them do not act independently. They are content to carry out their parents or their husbands behests Gandhi believed that in our society majority of women don't have much education and they don't aware what is going around the world which is the reason behind a good number of the evil practices persist against women. So education is important for women. No doubt he understood that education was essential to the proclamation of their natural rights, that of using them wisely and that they used them for personal gain. He stood up for the accurate education for women as she believed that after receiving an education they became more sensitive to the obvious inequalities they faced.

Barriers to Women's Education:

Physical, social, cultural, health, economic, religious, legal, political, administrative, and educational aspects, as well as programs run by governments, non-governmental organizations, and other organizations to address the problem of women's education. Gender discrimination continues in India and much remains to be done in the field of women's education in India. The male and female literacy gap is a simple indicator, and the male literacy rate is higher than that of women. Women thought only of the housewife and it was better to stay in the house (Bhat, 2015). Many restrictions on girls' learning still exist. Some of the barriers to women's education are social, based on the perception of gender equality and gender inequality while others are driven by gender concerns and economic challenges. The result of gender-based shaping and speculation that women are often more involved in programs related to their domestic role (Nair, 2010).

Gandhi on Status of Women:

Gandhi as a social reformist sought to reform the patriarchal nature of the Indian society which tried to confine women to the status of an inferior sex subordinate to their male counterparts. He has made remarkable contributions for the enhancement of the status of women in India and inspired the women of his period that boosted their morale and helped them to rediscover their self esteem. Gandhi could not reconcile himself to the idea that women had a low place in our society and were inferior to men in intelligence or wisdom. According to him both men and women are of equal rank and supplementary to each other and the existence of one was could not be justified without the other. He further believed that the way men influence the public life, the domestic life falls under the influence of women and therefore women should have as much autonomy in her own circle of influence as man has in his own. As Gandhi said, "Woman is the companion of man gifted with equal mental capacities. She has the right to participate in the activities of man and she has an equal right of freedom and liberty with him." Gandhi also suggested that women should cease to think that they were the creatures to satisfy the lust of man. He called upon women to realize themselves as independent human beings and decorate themselves with high qualities so that whole humanity was benefited. Gandhi said, "Man is born of woman, he is flesh of her and bone of her bone. Come to your own and deliver your message again." Gandhi wished that women should realize that they were not slaves and playthings of men, their whims and fancies but should try to come up to the standard of men and should copy what was best in them. In Young India, Gandhi wrote, "The future of India lies on your knees, for you will nurture the future generation. You can bring up the children of India to become simple God-fearing and brave men and women, or you can coddle them to be weaklings, unfit to brave the storms of life and used to foreign fineries which they would find it difficult in after life to discard."

Gandhi's Views on Women's Education

According to Gandhi education of women is an important factor which would lead to their empowerment and ensure their moral development and make them capable of occupying the same platform as that of men. Men and women are compliments to each other and that "the wife is not the husband's slave but his companion and his help-mate and an equal partner in all joys and sorrows- as free as the husband to choose her own path." Women have equal mental abilities as that of men and an equal right to freedom and hence, educating the women would uphold their natural rights. "The Mahatma's views on education are based on family ideals because he assumes that man is supreme in the extramural activities and that women are supreme in intra-mural activities."(Nandela) Hence education imparted to both men and women should be according to their pre-ordained stations in life.

Man and woman are of equal rank but they are not identical. They are a peerless pair being supplementary to one another; each helps the other, so that without the one the existence of the other cannot be conceived, and therefore it follows as a necessary corollary from these facts that anything that will impair the status of either of them will involve the equal ruin of them both. In framing any scheme of women's education this cardinal truth must be constantly kept in mind. Man is supreme in the outward activities of a married pair and therefore it is in the fitness of things that he should have a greater knowledge thereof. On the other hand, home life is entirely the sphere of woman and therefore in domestic affairs, in the upbringing and education of children, women ought to have more knowledge. Not that knowledge should be divided into watertight compartments, or that some branches of knowledge should be closed to any one; but unless courses of instruction are based on a discriminating appreciation of these basic principles, the fullest life of man and woman cannot be developed. As for illiteracy among the women, its cause is not mere laziness and inertia as in the case of men. A more potent cause is the status of inferiority with which an immemorial tradition has, unjustly branded her. Man has converted her into a domestic drudge and an instrument of his pleasure, instead of regarding her as his helpmate and 'better half'! The result is a semi-paralysis of our society. Woman has rightly been called the mother of the race. We owe it to her and to ourselves to undo the great wrong that we have done her. (Harijan, 18-2-1939)

Mahatma Gandhi, an advocate of a solid foundation for human beings was firm on giving free and compulsory elementary education to all. In Harijan of 9 October, 1937, he wrote that he was firmly in favor of the principle of free and compulsory education for India. He further wrote that at this level along with the training in any trade, their physical, mental and spiritual potentialities also be developed. Under present circumstances, I would like to add further that arrangements should be made for free and compulsory education to all up to the secondary level3without any discrimination of lineage, gender, creed, caste or sub-caste. The government should do this. I firmly believe that if Mahatma Gandhi had been with us today, he would have held the same opinion. Imparting of physical and mental training for the growth of good physique and mind and moral education for the formation of character and good conduct on the elementary and the secondary levels should be the priority

The importance of women's education in India

According to the International Encyclopedia on women (1999) various authors highlight the role of women's empowerment in education. As employment plays an important role in improving the status of women in society, the education of women is central to any women's empowerment program (Dominic and Jothi, 2012). Educating an Indian woman creates an important opportunity for social and economic development in India. An educated Indian woman will make a positive impact on Indian society by contributing positively to the national and social economy. An educated woman reduces the risk of her child dying before the age of five. The chances of domination are higher as an educated woman is more likely to marry at an older age than an uneducated woman.

Conclusion

India is in the 21st century and it is a call to the time to realize that discrimination, crime against women and sexism will always lead to violations of women's rights and an obstacle to women's empowerment. So it is a good time to follow and remember the golden names of Mahatma Gandhi. If his goal of non-violence is followed by all nations, discrimination against women will be reduced and where there is no discrimination, there will be no need to empower women. And this will automatically lead to the building of a just society based on equality and justice. Cultural factors play an important role in creating barriers to women's education. Some cultures do not approve of the education of women and girls, and they do not offer the opportunity and support for success. The contributions of women in the community are not ignored. When women are empowered, the whole family is empowered and this strengthens the whole community. We must encourage women in all walks of life to promote women's education at all levels, to establish gender equality through education and education, and to establish schools, colleges and universities. Educated women must enforce their social, social, political and economic rights. This will help to improve the overall balance of women in society

CHAPTER THREE

Women Education in Modern Society

Introduction:

What does it mean to be a woman? First of all, a woman is a mother, a wife, a daughter, a friend. The woman is sensitive but also strong. The woman exudes beauty, sensuality, love. There is a woman standing behind any successful man and she experiences every feeling along him.

Women are true heroes who fight for their purposes, who go through life with their heads up and who love to be respected and appreciated. They are good friends and have compassion for each other. They are mothers who fight for their children, who sacrifice themselves for them. Women are the smile, the finesse and the love in this world. They have enormous soul power. Most of the time, women prefer to ignore ranking themselves as personalities, because they are always taking care of the people around her. Without some education and encouragement, they devalue themselves, we decided to come to their aid and give them an educational base to help them fulfill their dreams and goals.

Education is one of the most critical areas of empowerment for women, as both the Cairo and Beijing conferences affirmed. It is also an area that offers some of the clearest examples of discrimination women suffer. Among children not attending school there are twice as many girls as boys, and among illiterate adults there are twice as many women as men. Offering girls basic education is one sure way of giving them much greater power -- of enabling them to make genuine choices over the kinds of lives they wish to lead. This is not a luxury. That women might have the chance of a healthier and happier life should be reason enough for promoting girls' education. However, there are also important benefits for society as a whole. An educated woman has the skills, information and self-confidence that she needs to be a better parent, worker and citizen.

An educated woman is, for example, likely to marry at a later age and have fewer children. Cross-country studies show that an extra year of schooling for girls reduces fertility rates by 5 to 10 per cent. And the children of an educated mother are more likely to survive. In India, for example, the infant mortality rate of babies whose mothers have received primary education is half that of children whose mothers are illiterate. An educated woman will also be more productive at work -- and better paid. Indeed, the dividend for educational investment is often higher for women than men. Studies from a number of countries suggest that an extra year of schooling will increase a woman's future earnings by about 15 per cent, compared with 11 per cent for a man.

Use of Education:

Women have a very in-distinctive position in our economy and are an indispensable part of the society. Yes, education and knowledge empower women. The only way a society or nation can move forward, and aspire to economic growth and development is not just through education- but especially education among the women citizens.

"To awaken the people, it is the women who must be awakened. Once she is on the move, the family moves, the village moves, the nation moves." - Pt. Jawaharlal Nehru

Education is a milestone of women empowerment because it enables them to respond to challenges, to confront their traditional role and change their life. Education is one of the ways to spread the message of women empowerment. Education not only educates a person but also helps her realize that she is a vital part to the society. Occupational achievement, self-awareness and satisfaction are among the many things that will be ensured by effective use of education. Guidance and counseling also provided through education, helps women select their jobs and build career paths. Education will help women to empower through the knowledge of science and technology to face the challenges of today's technological age. It also helps them in garnering information through the computer all over the world. Education not only educates a woman but enables her to take decisions and accept responsibilities at her home and outer world. Education helps a woman to understand her rights to equal treatment like a man in the society of this nation.

Women Education in Vedic Period:

Most females were allowed to pursue education without significant constraints in the Vedic period. Women's education, unlike in the subsequent periods was not neglected. Female scholars were also present during this period. The educators of this period had divided women into two groups - Brahmavadinis and Sadyodvahas. The former were life-long students of philosophy and theology. Sadyodvahas used to continue their studies until they got married. There were many women poets and philosophers, such as Apala, Ghosha and Visvavara.

Women Education in British Period:

1. The Church Missionary Society tasted greater success in South India. The first boarding school for girls came up in Tirunelveli in 1821. By 1840 the Scottish Church Society constructed six schools with roll strength of 200 Hindu girls. When it was mid-century, the missionaries in Madras had included under its banner, 8,000 girls. Women's employment and education was acknowledged in 1854 by the East Indian Company's Programme: Wood's Dispatch. Slowly, after that, there was progress in female education, but it initially tended to be focused on the primary school level and was related to the richer sections of society. The overall literacy rate for women increased from 0.2% in 1882 to 6% in 1947.

2. In western India, Jyotiba Phule and his wife Savitribai Phule became pioneers of female education when they started a school for girls in 1848 in Pune. In eastern India, apart from important contributions by eminent Indian social reformers like Raja Ram Mohan Roy, Ishwar Chandra Vidyasagar, John Elliot Drinkwater Bethune was also a pioneer in promoting women's education in 19th-century India. With participation of like-minded social reformers like Ramgopal Ghosh, Raja Dakshinaranjan Mukherjee and Pandit Madan Mohan Tarkalankar, he established Calcutta's (now Kolkata) first school for girls in 1849 called the secular Native Female School, which later came to be known as Bethune School. In 1879, Bethune College, affiliated to the University of Calcutta, was established which is the oldest women's college in Asia.

3. In 1878, the University of Calcutta became one of the first universities to admit female graduates to its degree programmes, before any of the British universities had later done the same. This point was raised during the Ilbert Bill controversy in 1883, when it was being considered whether Indian judges should be given the right to judge British

offenders. The role of women featured prominently in the controversy, where English women who opposed the bill argued that Bengali women, whom they stereotyped as "ignorant" and neglected by their men and that Indian men should therefore not be given the right to judge cases involving English women. Bengali women who supported the bill responded by claiming that they were more educated than the English women opposed to the bill and pointed out that more Indian women had degrees than British women did at the time.

Independence India:

After India attained independence in 1947, the University Education Commission was created to recommend suggestions to improve the quality of education. However, their report spoke against female education, referring to it as: "Women's present education is entirely irrelevant to the life they have to lead. It is not only a waste but often a definite disability." However, the fact that the female literacy rate was at 8.9% post-Independence could not be ignored. Thus, in 1958, a national committee on women's education was appointed by the government, and most of its recommendations were accepted. The cruxes of its recommendations were to bring female education on the same footing as offered for boys.

Soon afterwards, committees were created that talked about equality between men and women in the field of education. For example, one committee on differentiation of curriculum for boys and girls (1959) recommended equality and a common curricula at various stages of their learning. Further efforts were made to expand the education system, and the Education Commission was set up in 1964, which largely talked about female education, which recommended a national policy to be developed by the government. This occurred in 1968, providing increased emphasis on female education.

Current Policies:

Before and after Independence, India has been taking active steps towards women's status and education. The 86th Constitutional Amendment Act, 2001, has been a path-breaking step towards the growth of education, especially for females. According to this act, elementary education is a fundamental right for children between the ages of 6 and 14. The government has undertaken to provide this education free of cost and make it compulsory for those in that age group. This undertaking is more widely known as Sarva Shiksha Abhiyan (SSA).

Since then, the SSA has come up with many schemes for inclusive as well as exclusive growth of Indian education as a whole, including schemes to help foster the growth of female education. **The major schemes are the following:**

Mahila Samakhya Program: This program was launched in 1988 as a result of the New Education Policy (1968). It was created for the empowerment of women from rural areas especially socially and economically marginalized groups. When the SSA was formed, it initially set up a committee to look into this programme, how it was working and recommended new changes that could be made.

Kasturba Gandhi Balika Vidyalaya Scheme(KGBV): This scheme was launched in July, 2004, to provide education to girls at primary level. It is primarily for the underprivileged and rural areas where literacy level for females is very low. The schools that were set up have 100% reservation: 75% for backward class and 25% for BPL (below Poverty line) females.

National Programme for Education of Girls at Elementary Level (NPEGEL): This programme was launched in July, 2003. It was an incentive to reach out to the girls who the SSA was not able to reach through other schemes. The SSA called out to the "hardest to reach girls". This scheme has covered 24 states in India. Under the NPEGEL, "model schools" have been set up to provide better opportunities to girls.

Other educational routes

Newlyweds (women specifically) are educated on family planning, safe sex, and birth control in population control programs. In addition, the government has established rural health houses managed by local health workers. These health professionals travel to different areas in order to impart information about women's health and birth control.

Raising awareness

The Canadian start-up Decode Global has developed the mobile game Get Water!, a game for social change focusing on the water scarcity in India and the effect it has on girls' education, especially in slums and rural areas. In areas with no ready access to water, girls are often pulled out of school to collect water for their families.

Women Education in Modern Society:

After independence the scope for women increased and Women Education in Modern India widened. The period and after 1948 in India, highest priority was given to women education. Women Education in Modern India became the major concern for both the government and civil society as educated women can play a vital role in the development of the country. Thus there was a great upsurge in awareness regarding women's rights among all sections of society. Various developmental programmes and policies were introduced in order to improve the social status of women. Education is creditable as it is beneficial for women as this reduces female infant mortality and child mortality rates.

In India the educational system was modified and three-tier instruction process was developed. All citizens of India are offered the right to education and Women Education in Modern India was opened to a new vista. The structure of Indian education system came into being. Two important structures came into being: formal and Non-Formal Education programme. Various other educational programmes such as online education and distance education were also launched. The main aim of all the educational programmes is to make every girl child of the society literate.

At present, Women Education in Modern India has achieved a new height. Currently, the entrance of women in engineering, medical and other professional colleges is overwhelmingly elevated. Most of the professional colleges in the country keep thirty percent of the seats reserved for females. In urban India, girls are opened to a far wider scope then the rural girls.

In cultural reality, the women enjoyed a privileged position in the Vedic period. The women had special customs, rituals and spirituality, with which men were not allowed to interfere. In medieval period though women had to suffer because of various foreign interferences, yet in modern times the condition of women developed gradually. Moreover, Women Education in Modern India increased the intellectuality of the Indian women. Indian history produces famous women saints, healers and priests. For instance Andal, a 6th century A.D. sage and Jnanananda Ma of the 20th century have contributed to the society.

Conclusion:

India is now a leading country in the field of women's education. History of India is never blank of brave women however it is full of women philosophers like Gargi, Viswabara, Maritreyi (of Vedic age) and other famous women are like Mirabai, Durgabati, Ahalyabi, Laxmibai, etc. All the famous historical women in India are inspirations for women of this age. We never forget their contributions to the society and country.

Today the modern woman is totally different from what she used to be. She tries to constantly improve her position in society, she is preoccupied with her looks, and what is very important, she is trying to have a normal life without being constrained by anyone or anything. She has the right to express her opinion without fearing that someone will punish her for that. The modern woman wants good education and a blooming professional life, a way of life that allows her to have a baby and she can do it alone if she does not find the right man to support her. Over the years, there have been several women who are now considered to have made revolutionary changes in the global development. Strong and characterful have become role models and ideals for all feminine generations of all time. Everyone has noticed something different either that they have something to say, to accomplish, to show they have managed to mark forever the evolution of women in society.

CHAPTER FOUR

Education Status of Tribal Women in India

Introduction

Approximately 8.2% of the country's population is made up of tribal people, or adivasis as they are more commonly referred to as a sign of self-assertion. The central region of India and some areas of the north-east are where the tribal people are primarily concentrated. It appears that women's status is significantly better in tribal societies than it is in society at large. In India in 1991, there were 971 females for every 1000 males in the tribes, compared to 927 females in the general population.

In the tribal community, women make up 50% of the total population. In comparison to women in general society, women's status in tribal societies is generally better. Indian tribal women are preparing the food in the village in Orissa, India. The Indian Constitution assigns special status to the Scheduled Tribes. Scheduled Tribes, also known as adivasis, vanbasis, tribes, or tribals, make up about 8 percent of the Indian population. There are 573 Scheduled Tribes spread across the nation, each of which speaks a unique language that differs from the one that is predominant in the State in which they reside. In India, there are more than 270 of these languages. In India, there are 74. 6 million tribal people, according to the 2001 census. Undivided Madhya Pradesh has the most tribal residents (16.40 million), followed by Orissa (7 million) and Jharkhand (6. 6 million).

From the Margins to the Center, a study recently released by Sama Resource Group for Women and Health (2018), focuses on health disparities among tribal communities in a few districts in Chhattisgarh, Jharkhand, and Odisha. The National Human Rights Commission (NHRC) supported it, and it vehemently emphasises the connection between tribal communities' poor health and their marginalised status in the socioeconomic and political contexts.

Some of the main causes of the marginalisation of Adivasis include land alienation, loss of access to and control over forests, forced relocation due to development projects and a lack of adequate rehabilitation, and debt.

Socio-Economic Status

She appreciates having the freedom to choose her marriage. A tribal woman can easily get a divorce and remarry. She has a job, so she is self-sufficient financially.

Women may wed more than one husband in some tribal communities. Polygyny is the practise of a man taking multiple wives. Polyandry is the practise of one woman having multiple husbands. They frequently use bride prices as part of wedding ceremonies. Surprisingly, in some tribal societies, the groom is required to perform physical labour and serve at the wife's home if he is unable to pay the bride price.

A tribal woman can easily get a divorce and remarry. She has a good job, so she is largely self-sufficient financially. Though the Socioeconomic status of tribal women is very rich, their health and education status is that much poor in comparison to the national average.

Health Status of Tribal Women

Tribals have a very high infant mortality rate. Low health status in tribal women is caused by low nutritional status and a higher fertility rate.

In the tribal belt, a woman is regarded as healthy if she can have four or five children while also working in the fields.

The rural and tribal women in India encounter challenging health issues owing to a range of factors. Lack of access to quality healthcare, illiteracy, low socioeconomic status, nutritional deficiencies, and traditional beliefs are some of the contributing factors. Sexual and reproductive health are frequently harmed by extreme health neglect.

Tribal communities face the "triple burden" of disease. Apart from high rates of malnutrition and communicable diseases (TB, leprosy, HIV etc), the advent of rapid urbanisation, and changing lifestyles and environment, has led to a rise in non-communicable diseases as well (cancer, diabetes, and hypertension). These are both in addition to the burden of mental illness and subsequent addiction. In addition to this:

1. The reproductive health of women encompasses their holistic healthcare, including physical, mental, and social well-being.

2. Tribal women are mostly malnourished, and their daily intake of adequate nutrients continues to be much below the recommended standards. This has been a critical challenge adding to the health crisis in tribal regions.

3. The nutritional status of women reflects directly on their cultural practices and socio-economic situation. Malnutrition affects most women mainly during reproduction due to inadequate food consumption and lack of a nutrient-enriched diet.

4. Additionally, the cultural preference to bear sons results in a high fertility rate that is closely spaced. This leads to loss of nutrition from the body that can have an adverse impact during pregnancy and child delivery.

5. According to a study, women from rural areas between the age group of 15-24 years face a high risk of sexual and reproductive health outcomes, accounting for 41% of total maternal deaths.

Educational Status

Tribal women's low educational status is evident in their higher dropout rates, lower literacy rates, and lower school enrolment rates.

When considering the bigger picture, the low rate of literacy among tribal women across India serves as a stark reminder of the appalling situation facing STs in the nation. North-eastern states have led the way in embracing all STs, but the majority of large states are bewildered by the enormous literacy gap between all females and tribal women.

Tamil Nadu has a lot of catching up to do among the southern states. It stands out with the largest gap of 26.6%, according to the annual report of the Union Tribal Affairs Ministry, with the ST women's literacy rate hovering around 46.8%. lower than the 49.4% national average. The causes are widespread and include poverty, forced labour, early marriage, the absence of nearby schools, prejudice, and the indigenous population's nomadic lifestyle. With 71.1% and 53% respectively above the national average, Kerala and Karnataka stood out.

So what is the next step? State governments must implement programmes to bring tribal students into the classrooms and raise awareness of the value of education among STs, the majority of whom reside in distant villages. They should also implement the current Central programmes for ST students and make sure the money is distributed to those who are in need. Every school needs to monitor these students. Every citizen has a fundamental right to education, so using it as the main strategy to advance STs into the mainstream.

Conditions of Tribal women in India

The tribal women, constitute like any other social group, about half of the total population. The tribal women, as women in all social groups, are more illiterate than men.Role of women is not only of importance in economic activities, but her role in non-economic activities is equally important. The tribal women work very hard, in some cases even more than the men.

- Mitra and Singh write that discrimination against women, occupational differentiation, and emphasis on status and hierarchical social ordering that characterise the predominant Hindu culture are generally absent among the tribal groups.
- Bhasin (2007) also writes that though tribes too have son preference, they do not discriminate against girls by female infanticide or sex determination tests.
- The status of tribal women can be judged mainly by the roles they play in society. Their roles are determined to a large extent through the system of descent.
- Most of the tribes in India follow a patrilinear system. There are exceptional cases like the Khasi, Jaintia, Garo and Lalung of Meghalaya in the North-East who follow the matrilineal system. The Mappilas of Kerala too are a matrilineal community.

Women in tribal communities put in a lot of work, so they are valued as assets. Unsurprisingly, they frequently pay a bride price during marriages. The tribal women in the North East were well known for their weaving abilities. The majority of tribal girls used to learn how to weave at home. Tribal women, as a result, have very little control over immovable property. They typically used to weave in their free time and for self-consumption. Land is rarely passed down to them, especially in patrilineal societies.

Problems faced by tribal women

1. Despite several economic, political and social changes, women, are still far behind.
2. Primitive Economy results in overburdening of women. They are exposed to wild animals, poisonous vegetation as a cost of survival

(women are known to actively participate in economy)

3. Cultural Practices – Numerous practices like genital mutilation are disastrous to the physical and mental health of women.
4. Health: Malnutrition, anaemia, lack of access to healthcare & proper medicines, lack of literacy & education opportunities, low empowerment & sense of independence
5. Sexual Exploitation – A number of complaints regarding officials committing sexual offences have come to light. (especially Naxalite area)
6. Isolation – Prevents women to take up education or benefit from government policies like maternity benefit, reservation etc.
7. Financial exploitation by money lenders.
8. Male migration leading to feminization of agriculture and poverty.
9. Tribal migrant women face issues of low wages, bad work conditions, malnutrition, unhygienic sanitation, cramped housing.

Conclusion

Tribal feminism and philosophical feminism are divided in the West based on ideals. However, in states like Jharkhand, Chattisgarh, the seven sisters of the North East, Odisha, and others with a high concentration of tribal people, feminism is not divided by mere denomination but is instead unified by the ideology of achieving equality in both public and private spheres. There have been significant progressive changes in the tribal community in recent years after much deliberation. Both men and women are being impacted by modernization as it takes over. Men are still viewed as more deserving than women, however, because of the weight of unfair sociocultural norms and gender roles.and frequently by us as women. It's time to shine a spotlight on these tribal women and provide them with a stage to do so.

CHAPTER FIVE

The Fight Against Triple Talaq

INTRODUCTION

The word talaq typically means "repudiation" or just "divorce." It refers to the husband's right, in classical Islamic law, to dissolve marriages by simply telling her that his wife is repudiating or divorcing her.

Divorce in Islam named 'talaq,' meaning "I divorce you" when a woman asks her husband 'talaq,' the word could be translated as 'divorce me, please! "Most non-Muslims consider a Muslim (married) to have the capacity at all times to dissolve marriage by saying to his wife: 'Talaq, talaq, talaq.' Even that is not easy or easy in Islam, as different procedures must be performed in compliance with the rules of Islamic law as a form of obligation between the two parties.

Under Islamic law, there are three types of divorce: Talaq-e-Ahsan, Talaq-e-Hasan and Talaq-e-Biddat.

- **Talaq-e-Ahsan:**

Talaq-e-Ahsan is the most ideal way of dissolving a marriage. "Ahsan" means the best or the right thing to do. In accordance with Talaq e-Ahsan, when the wife is 'pure,' that is, not menstrual, the husband must make a divorce in one sentence.

After talaq has been pronounced, the wife must follow a time of iddats, waiting and abstinence. The iddat cycle for menstrual women and for pregnant women is three months, before they have been born.

If the couple re-establishes coexistence or affection, the proclamation is considered as withdrawn during the time of iddat. "Talaq-e-ahsan" is therefore repeal able. In comparison, if there is no restart of coexistence or intimacy, the time of 'iddat' would mean that after the expiration of the iddat era the divorce is final and irrevocable.

- **Talaq-e-Hasan:**

The husband pronounces talaq three times in three monthly courses under Talaq-e-Hasan, a "proper" means of divorce but not as well as Ahsan.

Following the first declaration of divorce, the declaration of divorce shall be dealt with by revoking the statement of divorce if cohabitation is resumed within a span of one month.

In the first one there is only one declaration of 'talaq' and then abstinence during the time of 'iddat,' while in the second one of three pronouncements of 'talaq' are combined with abstinence. There are three words of 'talaq' which are not mixed with the same pronunciation.

- **Talaq-e-Biddat:**

Talaq-e-biddat, prohibited in August by the Supreme Court, is viewed as unacceptable or 'sinful' to Islam but still applicable in accordance with the Sharia law. Such an immediate divorce is a unusual thing rather than the norm within Islam.

Biddat means sinful creativity-Ommeyad's kings have adopted this type in order to overcome the rule. The husband pronounces talaq three times in one position under this form of divorce. Divorce is immediate and immediately irrevocable, regardless of iddat. It cannot therefore be revoked once pronounced.

What is Triple Talaq?

Triple Talaq, therefore, is the norm in which a Muslim man can divorce his wife by simply three times uttering "talaq." In other words, as it is known, "Triple talaq" allows a husband to divorce his wife by repeating three times in any form, including email or text message, the term "talaq" (divorce).

Triple talaq is also known as "Talaq-e-Biddat". "Biddat" means some invention, and Muhammad (Prophet) spoke of biddat as follows:

In this regard, Muhammad (Prophet) says: "He who innovates something that is not in accordance with our matter (religion), will have it rejected." Even Allah says that biddat in Islam is not permissible in the interpretation of the context of the Holy Quran. [Holy Quran5:4(2)] The worst part of talaq-ul-biddat is that the divorce comes into force when a person utters the words of "Talaq." The Prophet Muhammad never agreed to this form of talaq. In chapters No.2, 4 and 65, the Holy Quran explicitly states that

Muslim men have to wait until the end of the iddat (waiting period) period, and hence disapprove of the talaq (divorce) in one go.

The root of Talaq-ul-biddat dates from the second century of the Islamic period. The second caliph Umar imposed triple divorce after two years of ruling, according to which no one would be able to take back his wife after pronouncing three divorces in one go.

A topic of controversy and debate has been the use and status of triple talaq in India. Issues of justice, gender equality, human rights and secularism have been raised by those questioning the practise. Issues of justice, gender equality, human rights and secularism have been raised by those questioning the practise. The Government of India and the Supreme Court of India have been active in the debate and are related to the debate in India concerning the Uniform Civil Code (Article 44). The Indian Supreme Court ruled instant triple talaq (talaq-e-biddat) unconstitutional on 22 August 2017. Triple talaq is considered to be an especially unapproved but legally legitimate form of divorce in traditional Islamic jurisprudence.

What is Triple Talaq Act?

The Muslim Women (Protection of Rights on Marriage) Act, 2019 is an Act of the Parliament of India criminalising triple talaq. In August 2017, the Indian Supreme Court ruled triple talaq to be unconstitutional, allowing Muslim men to divorce their wives instantly. The opinion of the minority proposed that Parliament deem the required laws regulating triple talaq in the Muslim community.

On 27 December 2018, the Lok Sabha passed the 2017 resolution. In the Rajya Sabha, however, the opposition requested that it be referred to the Standing Committee. An order that made the bill effective expired on 22 January 2019, as the bill was not passed in the parliamentary session. On 10 January 2019, the government re-promulgated an identical draught law. In the Lok Sabha, this bill was passed but was again stalled in the Rajya Sabha. The bill lapsed again when in April 2019 the Legislative session adjourned sine die.

The Muslim Women (Protection of Rights on Marriage) Ordinance, 2019 was set to expire after the 2019 Indian general elections on 29 August 2019, six weeks after the beginning of the parliamentary session. On 21 June 2019, in the Lok Sabha, the government introduced a new bill. It was passed on 25 July 2019 by the Lok Sabha and on 30 July 2019 by the Rajya Sabha. On 31 July 2019, the President, Ram Nath Kovind, signed the bill. It was subsequently published on the same day in the Gazette. As of 19 September

2018, the act is retrospectively effective.

The Muslim Women (Protection of Rights on Marriage) Bill, 2017

After the Supreme Court judgement in August 2017 barring triple talaq in India, the government formulated the bill alleging 100 instant triple talaq cases. The Muslim Women (Protection of Rights on Marriage) Bill, 2017, was passed by the Lok Sabha on 28 December 2017. In any manner, spoken, in writing or through electronic means such as email, SMS and instant messengers, the bill proposed to make triple talaq illegal and void, with up to three years in prison for the husband who pronounces triple talaq. The bill was opposed by the Communist Party of India (Marxist), Rashtriya Janata Dal, All India Majlis-e-Ittehadul Muslimeen, Biju Janata Dal and the Indian Union Muslim League, calling it arbitrary and flawed, although the bill was endorsed by the Indian National Congress.

The Muslim Women (Protection of Rights on Marriage) Bill, 2018

The Muslim Women's (Protection of Marriage Rights) Bill (2018) was later introduced to protect Muslim women. The bill was passed by the Lok Sabha in 2018 and 2019, but lapsed after the Rajya Sabha refused to pass it.

On 19 September 2018, the government issued The Muslim Women (Protection of Rights on Marriage) Ordinance, 2018, noting that the practise of instant triple talaq had continued unabated despite the 2017 judicial mandate. If either the Parliament does not approve it within six weeks of reassembly or if disapproving resolutions are passed by both houses, an ordinance brought into the Indian parliament lapses. Therefore, the Union Law Minister, Ravi Shankar Prasad, introduced a new bill called The Muslim Women (Protection of Rights on Marriage) Bill, 2018 in the Lok Sabha.**The Muslim Women (Protection of Rights on Marriage) Bill, 2019**

On July 31, 2019, when the bill was passed by both houses of the legislature, Lok Sabha and Rajya Sabha, and notified by the President of India in the official gazette, the Muslim Women (Protection of Rights on Marriage) Ordinance, 2019 was repealed and thus became an Act of Parliament. There are 8 parts of the Act.

In various Muslim nations in the world, the Triple Talaq was abolished, which is given as follows:

- Pakistan
- Egypt
- Tunisia

- Sri Lanka
- Bangladesh
- Turkey
- Indonesia
- Iraq

As a matter of interest, are we going to talk about why it is mandatory to abolish triple talaq? Why is there a need to pass the law's triple talaq bill? So, the answer is here. Since it is un-Quranic, triple talaq should be abolished; it goes against the spirit of the Constitution and, lastly, but most significantly, it is unfair and cruel.

After being orally divorced in an instant, women were made homeless overnight, leaving destitute with no support for the children either. Many women experience life-long trauma and find it hard to recover from the shock. Some also came to the public hearings in Delhi and gave testimony in person. In most instances, when the husband pronounced talaq thrice, the women were not even present. Some of them narrated how some of the current religious bodies they approached did not find support.

It is obvious, legally speaking, that triple talaq is a gross violation of women citizens ' rights. The right to religious freedom extends to women and men in equal measure. It never gives permission to male people to exploit female citizens. Leading to misinterpretations and intervention by patriarchal Orthodox bodies, Muslim women have been denied their Quranic privileges.

ANALYSIS AND DISCUSSION

After triple talaq, married Muslim women find themselves socially as well as economically vulnerable and insecure. Some people say it's nice to ban triple talaq, while some say the opposite. What is the view of people in support of triple talaq, what are the circumstances of triple talaq that will be studied and debated here before and after the enactment of the bill?

The 5 Women who led the fight against Triple Talaq

There is the list of women who fight against the Triple Talaq:

a. **Shayara Bano**

After her husband of 15 years sent her a letter with talaq written three times and left her, Shayara Bano of Uttarakhand first approached the top court. Petitions were tagged with Ms Bano's petition by four other women.

The sixth petitioner in the case is the Bharatiya Muslim Mahila Andolan (BMMA).

a. Ishrat Jahan

Ishrat Jahan, of Howrah, West Bengal, was divorced by phone from her husband. Murtaza, her 15-year-old husband, called from Dubai in April 2015, said 'talaq, talaq, talaq' and disconnected.

c. Gulshan Parveen

When she visited her parents in 2015, Gulshan Parveen of Rampur in Uttar Pradesh received a talaqnama or divorce notice on a Rs10/- stamp document. "My husband felt like it one fine day and suddenly both my two-year-old son Ridan and I were homeless," said Ms Parween. She declined to consider the notice, during which the family court was approached by her husband.

d. Aafreen Rehman

After meeting her husband via a marriage portal, Aafreen Rehman got married in 2014. "After two-three months, my in-laws began to mentally torment me and demand dowry," she was quoted as saying by the ANI news agency. "Later they even started beating me and in September 2015 they asked me to leave their house." Rehman got three times talaq from her husband in January 2016, in a letter sent by speed mail. The Supreme Court came to her later.

e. Atiya Sabri

Atiya Sabri, married in 2012, on a piece of paper, was also divorced. In January, she approached the Supreme Court to appeal her divorce.

Provisions under the Muslim Women (Protection of Rights on Marriage) Act, 2019

- Any pronouncement of a talaq on his wife by a Muslim husband, by words, either spoken or written or in electronic form or in any other way, shall be void and unlawful.

- Any Muslim husband who pronounces talaq against his wife shall be punished by imprisonment for a term of up to three years, as well as a fine.
- A married Muslim woman upon whom talaq is pronounced shall be entitled to receive from her husband, as determined by the Magistrate, the amount of the subsistence allowance for her and dependent children.
- A married Muslim woman shall, in the event of a declaration of talaq by her husband, be entitled to custody of her minor children in such a manner as may be decided by the Magistrate.
- An offence punishable under this Act shall be recognisable where information relating to the commission of the offence is provided to the officer in charge of the police station by a Muslim woman married to whom talaq is pronounced or by any person connected with her by blood or marriage;
- In the case of a married Muslim woman on whom talaq is pronounced with the approval of the Magistrate, an offence punishable under this Act shall be compoundable under such terms and conditions as may be decided.
- No person accused of an offence punishable under this Act shall be released on bail unless the Magistrate is satisfied that there are appropriate grounds for granting bail to such person on an application submitted by the accused and after hearing the married Muslim woman upon whom talaq is pronounced.

How much Freedom did the Triple Talaq Bill bring for Muslim Women?

Banda (Uttar Pradesh): Subi Begum was waiting outside the civil court of Banda to hear a case against which she had been struggling for years. I feel at ease when I think a husband will not give a talaq at whim right now. He must be aware of the implications and will think twice,' she said.

Subi is a Muslim woman who, contrary to the wishes of her family, married a Hindu man only to discover his violent features later. He would constantly threaten, taking advantage of her Muslim identity, to give her an instant talaq, which she refused to accept. Finding herself stuck with nowhere to go, she was permitted to live in a separate room with her daughter in her in-law's house after many negotiations.

Does SC declare Triple Talaq unconstitutional; Good verdict, bad law?

In July 2019, the Supreme Court ruled "triple talaq" unconstitutional, a form of divorce practised by Muslims in India that allows a man to terminate his marriage by uttering the word "talaq" three times in literary, oral or electronic media.

In its judgement, the court noted that triple talaq had also been made unconstitutional by Muslim majority nations such as Saudi Arabia and Pakistan and ordered the Centre's Prime Minister Narendra Modi-led government to enact a banning bill.

Although the proposal to end "triple talaq" was sponsored by many Muslims, including women's rights organisations and religious leaders, as they considered it unconstitutional and irreligious, there was also strong opposition to it.

The All India Muslim Personal Law Board rejected the decision, claiming that a community's religious traditions were not interfered with by the court and that the proportion of divorce in Muslims was much lower than in other groups.

The clause in the Bill to make instant divorce a criminal offence among Muslim men was the biggest bone of contention. This clause became the key source of contention between the ruling Bharatiya Janata Party, keen to reap electoral gains from the Muslim community, and the opposition, who wanted the Bill referred to a Parliamentary Committee, as the Muslim Women (Protection of Rights on Marriage) Bill was passed in the Lok Sabha on December 27.

Triple talaq reactions across the nation

Rajya Sabha's decision to approve The Muslim Women (Marriage Rights Protection) Bill, 2019 has received positive responses from across the political and social spectrum. As a historic moment for the country, the NDA government has hailed the passage of the bill.

In the opinions shared by many Muslim women as they welcomed the historic passage of the triple talaq bill by parliament, the emotions were palpable and very obvious.

Union Minister Smriti Zubin Irani said that by spearheading the bill in parliament, the government led by Prime Minister Narendra Modi had developed a social and political history.

Triple Talaq: Muslim women happy over Supreme Court judgment

There were mixed reactions from citizens in Lucknow to the verdict of the Supreme Court banning the practice of Triple Talaq for six months among Muslims. Until now, by saying 'Talaq' three times, men could immediately leave their wives. Women were content in the minority community and called it their 'victory'. Some of the reactions are given here;

a. Dr Shirin of AMU, Aligarh, a Triple Talaq victim:

This is our victory. It would have been better had the judgment been unanimous. All those women who have suffered the pang of separation because of no fault of theirs are very happy now.

"My husband wrote three dreaded words in a letter and sent it to me and the Qazi justified the talaq. I have a four-year-old daughter. I do not want any financial help but the judgment has given me mental relief," she said.

"Though my daughter asks where her father is, I will not re-marry. I now know the meaning of marriage and the value of a husband. In Islam, a wife is treated as a door mat. I do not want to be treated as a doormat anymore," she said.

b. All India Muslim Women Personal law Board chief Shaista Ambar:

This is a historic judgment which will give a new lease of life to women who were divorced in this manner. Some clerics interfered with Islam and gave their wrong interpretation of Islamic laws by justifying Talaq in one sitting. The court has called this interference as unconstitutional.

Islam has an elaborate procedure to end marriages. This spreads over three months. We expect the government to ratify a law in six months. I am sure the new law will guarantee equal rights for women.

c. Eidgah Aishbagh's Imam Maulana Khalid:

I have reservation on the SC's direction to the government to bring a law on Talaq. The government law could be interference in our personal law which has been protected by the Constitution.

As per Shariat law, Triple Talaq is valid if Islamic procedure is followed. We are also in favour of abolition of Triple Talaq at one go. This should end but there should not be any interference with our personal law.

d. All India Muslim Personal Law Board (AIMPLB) member Zafaryab Jilani:

The Board has called a meeting on September 10 to deliberate on the issue of Triple Talaq. The AIMPLB itself considers Talaq at one go as a crime. We will suggest that Qazis, while solemnising marriages, should tell the newlyweds that divorce at one go is a crime in the eye of the Allah.

The judgment is very confusing as some say the court has asked the government to bring a law within six months. But the Board will not allow any interference in the personal law of Muslims.

However few political leaders also maintained the courtesy of representing the men's side opinion on triple talaq:

AIMIM MP Asaduddin Owaisi, opposing the triple talaq bill in the Lok Sabha, questioned why the Centre wants to criminalise triple talaq since homosexuality has been decriminalised by the Supreme Court.

It notes that triple talaq has already been ruled unconstitutional by the Supreme Court's judgement in Shayara Bano v/s Union of India (2017). What are you punishing your husband for then?

Civil society members said that the bill was a "complete charade" and said that they would ask President Ram Nath Kovind to persuade him not to sign it into law. "The declaration read," We the undersigned organisations and individuals reject the government's attempt to criminalise Muslim men in the guise of protecting Muslim women. Today we stand in firm opposition to the Muslim Women (Protection of Marriage Rights) Bill, 2019, which this government has forced through the Rajya Sabha in great haste. Why hasn't it been referred to a select committee?

The bill was opposed by MPs from RJD, AIMIM, BJD, AIADMK, and AIML, calling it arbitrary in nature and a flawed plan, though Congress supported the bill tabled by law minister Ravi Shankar Prasad in the Lok Sabha. In the Lok Sabha, 19 amendments were moved, but all were rejected.

RECOMMENDATIONS AND FINDINGS

Examination of the current status of Muslim women in the country in the light of some of the recommendations made by law following the abolition of Triple Talaq. Women were content in the minority community and called it their 'victory'. Some reactions are described here:

a. **Shayara Bano**

"It is a happy moment for not just me but for Muslim society as a whole. We have been freed of an evil custom," said Shayara Bano, the first petitioner in the case. "Generations of women have suffered due to instant triple talaq. They have been thrown out of their house overnight and made to go through hell. Why is everyone still concerned about the men and not about the women," she said.

She said a Bill was necessary since, even after the Supreme Court's order, the practice of instant triple talaq continued. "There were so many cases despite the SC order. There was no fear among people. This law will instill that fear," said Bano, who lives in Kashipur in Uttarakhand.

Bano, who was given triple talaq in 2015, said that while she has won the larger cause, she is still waging her personal battle for rights to see her two children more often and for maintenance from her husband. "My husband has remarried now. He has turned my son and daughter, now teenagers, against me. The only time I get to see them is when they are brought to the Kashipur family court once in three months," she said.

b. Zakia Soman

"This has been long overdue. It has come late but, nevertheless, it is a welcome development. However, a comprehensive reform in Muslim personal law is called for. But even one step is welcome," said Zakia Soman of the Bharatiya Muslim Mahila Andolan (BMMA), a vociferous advocate of the abolition of triple talaq.

BMMA's petition was suo motu turned into a PIL by a two-judge bench of the Supreme Court before Shayara Bano's case against instant triple talaq was filed. That petition eventually became one of six.

c. Ishrat Zehan

"This is great news... My life has been ruined, but no other woman's life will be ruined now... They will not have to undergo the hardship that I faced... The law is on our side now," said Ishrat Zehan.

"After giving me talaq over the phone, my husband abandoned me. My children were taken away. When I filed a petition in the Supreme Court, a section of my neighbours turned against me. Even now, they threaten to throw me out of my house and the neighbourhood. My battle is still going on," said Zehan, who lives in Howrah.

"The law will give relief to thousands of women. It is historic," said Zehan, who joined the BJP in January 2018.

Jehan got married in 2001, when she was just 14. In April 2015, her husband called her up from Dubai and said talaq thrice. He later remarried.

d. Gulshan Parveen

"My life is still where it was five years ago, when I was asked to leave my husband's house," said Gulshan Parveen, who approached Shayara Bano's lawyers in 2015, after her husband sent her a talaqnama. Her husband remarried, and Gulshan moved back to Delhi from Uttar Pradesh. She has been since struggling to make ends meet for herself and her five-year-old son.

"I have no job since all my documents are still with my former in-laws. The Supreme Court case is long over but I am fighting two separate cases in the lower courts, including one of domestic violence. The monthly maintenance amount I have been awarded is a mere Rs6000/-, which is barely enough to even cover my child's fees," she said.

She feels that the law is much needed for the sake of the "dignity of Muslim women". "The government has only outlawed talaq-e-biddat (instant triple talaq). Men still have the upper hand and can pronounce talaq to their wives and unilaterally divorce them over a period of three months (talaq-e-ahsan). The power still vests with the man," she said.

e. Aafreen Rehman

"I am very happy today... it's a historic win for us. We cannot change whatever happened to me, but we now have a way to stop this practice which has been going on for centuries," said Aafreen Rehman from Jaipur. She said the provision of jail term would "scare the men" and make them think twice about giving triple talaq.

In January 2016, Rehman was given triple talaq by her husband, in a letter sent through speed post. She later approached the Supreme Court.

CONCLUSION

The abolition of the Triple Talaq Bill is one of the most important findings that no Muslim will face such prejudice or oppression in their future lives. The new amendment to the Triple Talaq Act is really an incentive for India's women's empowerment movement. It is in this sense that Muslim women will be able to live in society with social and economic security and with honour and dignity after the implementation of the Act.

In the Muslim world, the court has given progressive thoughts on personal rule. The abolition of Triple Talaq would, in the future, deny prejudice and inequality in the lives of Muslim women. Against this social evil, society should also come forward to abolish this activity. Since women's empowerment is very important for the nation's development, particularly with regard to taking an active role in the decision-making processes.

CHAPTER SIX

Government Initiatives for Women's Empowerment

Introduction

Women empowerment refers to spiritual, political, social, educational, gender or economic strengths of Individual communities of women. It means growing their potential for strength and decision making so that they can assist in society's development and stand equal to men. The empowerment of women is a necessary tool to develop the country and achieve the aim of growth.

Women's empowerment traditionally encompasses all steps taken to increase the status of women by various means, such as schooling, awareness-raising, literacy, and training. Therefore, their empowerment is all about adorning and empowering women to have the right to make choices that decide life by overcoming all the obstacles of the cruel society.

The empowerment of women is all about equipping and empowering women through the multiple problems in society to make life-determining choices. Women's empowerment can't be noticed in a day. It's a system where various minutes change swill lead to huge change in the society. However, women empowerment is now considered as the growth strategies along with the overall economic and development prosperity in most of countries around the world.

Women empowerment refers to a woman's ability to make her own decisions, control her own time and money and not being dependent on men to fulfil her wishes. Women should be able to live her life unapologetically and according to her own will and wishes. In India, the rate of women empowerment has been quite slow due to the male dominant nature of society prevailing since the time of independence and even way before that. Women are taught to be fragile, compromise and what not.

Empowerment for women in India needs a crosscutting approach, something that puts light on the diversity of social structures that women's lives plays around.

Importance of women empowerment

It is important to stimulate women's confidence by giving them all the possibilities within their ability so that they can see the abilities they have and are latent within them. Women's empowerment aims to foster women's faith by supplying them with all they can to help them see the skills they have that are latent inside them. Only through better schooling, knowledge and a space to freely express oneself is it possible to properly nurture, polish and sharpen those skills.

In countering this backwardness, women's empowerment plays a critical role in the ways below.

- **Recognising that women are equally capable**

It is important to realise and recognise that women are not only equally competent in the modern era, but also ahead of men in many socio-economic fields, making their presence extremely significant on the job front.

- **Women's requirement at working place**

Indeed, some occupations are unable to achieve their best potential without women's participation. In order to accomplish the ideals they strive to achieve, female presence is crucial for the smooth running of the system.

- **Development of a society**

Women's empowerment is a requirement for the growth of a community, as it increases both the quality and the amount of human capital available for growth.

- **Sustainable development of the country.**

Without gender equality and women's empowerment, sustainable development is unlikely. The full participation of both males and females is widely believed to be critical for growth. Just understanding the role of men would not be beneficial for sustainable growth.

The empowerment of women aims to give women economic freedom and to contribute to the economic gains of households and society as a whole.WomenEmpowerment is very important in the contemporary times since there exists unequal power relations between men and women in every sphere of life.

Steps taken by the government for women's empowerment

• Beti Bachao Beti padhao yojana

Beti Bachao Beti padhao yojana was launched on 22 January 2015 by current Prime Minister Narendra Modi. It aims to address the issue of the declining child sex ratio image (CSR) and is a national initiative jointly run by Ministry of Women and Child Development, the Ministry of Health and Family Welfare and the Ministry of Finance. It's a campaign of Government of India that aims to generate awareness and improve the efficiency of welfare services intended for girls in India. It initially focused multi-sector action in 100 districts throughout the country where there was a low CSR.

• Mahila-E-Haat

The Indian Government launched the Mahila-E-Haat program in 2016 under the Ministry of Women and Child Development. It's an initiative for meeting aspirations and needs of women entrepreneurs. Women can display their products through online Marketing platform. This initiative is a part of "Digital India" and "Stand up" initiatives. It seeks to support aspiring women entrepreneurs, self-help organisations, and NGOs by leveraging technology to make it easier for platforms to showcase and reach a broader audience with their goods and services.

• Mahila Shakti Kendra

The Indian Government launched the Mahila Shakti Kendra program in 2017. It aims to empower rural women through community participation and to create an environment in which they realize their full potential. It will provide an interface for rural women to approach the government for availing their entitlements also empowering them through training and capacity building. This program is working through community engagement through student volunteers in the 115 most backward districts of India.

- Support to training and employment program for women(STEP)

The STEP Scheme aims to provide skills and competencies that enable women to become self employed/entrepreneur. This program also includes providing accurate competencies and training for women. The scheme is intended to benefit women who are in the age group of 16 years and above across the country.

- Working Women Hostel scheme

Working Women Hostels is introduced by the Government of India in order to ensure the safety of working women who live away from home. These hostels provide working families with comfortable accommodation, as well as day care facilities for their children, and these hostels are set up wherever possible, whether in urban, semi-urban or rural areas.

Types of woman empowerment

a. Political Empowerment

Political empowerment exists when women are given a fair representation in politics such as having their voices heard in the mainstream media and giving their views and opinions regarding policies and programs to be implemented. Political empowerment encourages the adoption of policies that will better foster gender equality and agency for women in both the public and private spheres.The full and equitable participation of women in public life is essential to building and sustaining strong, vibrant democracies. Women throughout the world have been struggling to break away the shackle of bondage, subjugation, oppression and all kinds of ill treatment both within and outside of their families. Without bringing them in the corridor of power where they can formulate policies and programs and implement them, the survival of women is very difficult.

a. Economic Empowerment

Economic empowerment occurs when women have complete control over their hard earned finances and have a right to spend them in a way in which they wish to. Through employment women earn money and it enables women and girls to become 'bread earners', contributing members of households with the strong sense of their own economic independence. Economic empowerment is a powerful weapon against poverty. Around 2 billion poor people around the world – particularly women – are financially excluded and women and girls make up the majority of the poorest people in the world today. Women continue to earn on average only 60 to 75% of what men earn.

c. Educational Empowerment

Educational empowerment occurs when a fair opportunity is given to girls and women to attain education. Education is of prime importance because it gives a sense of confidence and self esteem to women. Women have a very in-distinctive position in our economy and are an indispensable part of the society. Education is a milestone of women empowerment because it enables them to respond to challenges, to confront their traditional role and change their life. Not only does education educate a girl, but it also allows her to understand that she is a critical part of society. Among the many aspects that can be ensured by successful use of education are occupational achievement, self awareness and satisfaction.

d. Social empowerment

Social Empowerment refers to the enabling force that strengthens women's social relations and their position in social structures. Social empowerment addresses the social discriminations existing in the society based on disability, race, ethnicity, religion, or gender.

Principles of women empowerment

1. Establish High Level corporate leadership for gender equality.
2. Treat all women and men fairly at work – respect and support human rights and non discrimination
3. Ensure the health, safety and well-being of all women and men workers.
4. Promote education, training and professional development for women.

5. Implement enterprise development, supply chain and marketing practices that empower. Women.
6. Promote equality through community initiatives and advocacy.
7. Measure and publicly report on progress to achieve gender equality.

Status of Women in India

"Woman has been suppressed under custom and law for which man was responsible and in the shaping of which she had no hand woman has as much right to shape her own destiny as man has to shape his It is up to men to see that they enable them to realize their full status and play their part as equal of men"

Mahatma Gandhi

In India, since long back, women were considered as an oppressed section of the society and they were neglected for centuries. In Vedic age, the women were declared to be innately unfit for independence. Since time immemorial, they have been subject to torture, mal-treatment and all sorts of misbehaviour. Western impact influenced the Indian social-system and era of social reforms began during the 19century. The Sati tradition was eliminated, slave trade abolished, girls education started and in the eyes of law women were provided equal status. While in pre-independence India, education among women was slow and limited to upper strata of society it tremendously increased in independent India. The first task in post-independent India was to provide a constitution to the people, which would not make any distinctions on the basis of sex. Article 15(1) of the Indian Constitution guarantees equalities of opportunities for all citizens in matters of employment. Article 15(3) provides that the state can make any special provisions for women and children. Besides, directive principle of state policy which concern women directly and have a special bearing on their status directly and have a special bearing on their status include Article 39(a) right to an adequate means of livelihood; (d) equal pay for equal work both men and women, (e) protection of health and strength of workers men, women, children and Article 42 provides for just and humane conditions of work and maternity relief.

Women empowerment in rural v/s urban

A community based cross-sectional study was conducted during June 2018 among the ruralgroup in Nandivaram village in Kancheepuram, Rural Health training Centre

and urban group in Shenoy Nagar (UHTC) attached to Government Kilpauk Medical College, Tamil Nadu. The study population comprised of women in reproductive

age group (15-45 years) residing in the study area. Only married women in the study area who were willing to participate in this study were included. Sample size was

estimated to be 200 in each group using the proportion of women taking part in household decision making reported as 84% in NFHS-4 for the state of Tamil Nadu.

Women empowerment is vital for decision making on nutrition, health-seeking, family planning and economic issues for the family as a whole. In reality, there is prevalence of unequal gender norms among the women in India in urban and rural areas.

Role of women empowerment in different states

• Women access to money, credit and freedom of movement.

Percentage of women age (15-49) who have money, bank or savings accounts that they themselves can use, have taken a loan from micro-credit programme and are allowed to go to their specified places alone are considered in our analysis. High levels of women access to money, credit and freedom of movement are favourable. Union territories like Goa (269.6), Chandigarh (269.0), have high scores in women access to money, credit and freedom of movement as compared to other states like Tamil Nadu (236.2), Sikkim (234.8), whereas states like Bihar (68.2), Nagaland (71.5), Manipur (79.6) are under performers in this indicator.

• Participation of women in decision making

Percentage of women between age (15-49) who make major household purchases and

are independent to visit her family and relatives were considered. High level of female autonomy is good, therefore making it a positive indicator to measure women empowerment. States like Bihar (3.6), Haryana (8.5) and Union territories like Delhi (13.8) are the underperformers in participation of women in decision making whereas states like Nagaland (200), Sikkim (189.8), Mizoram (167), are the states with highest scores in participation of women in decision making.

Women empowerment during corona pandemic

As the current COVID-19 global pandemic spreads through the world, the UN Trust Fund to End Violence against Women (UN Trust Fund), and its grantees, recognize the gender dimensions of the impact from the COVID-19 outbreak. In this challenging time, the need to respond to the immediate and long-term consequences of the current crisis for women and girls is critical.

Two recent reports highlight the uneven economic impact of the Covid-19 pandemic on men and women. First, an informal workers' survey conducted by Action Aid Association between May and June covering 20 Indian states shows more women were out of work post-lockdown compared to men. In fact, by mid-May, 79% of the women surveyed reported they were unemployed compared to 75% of men. Additionally, 51.6% of the women reported no wages during the lockdown period compared to 46% of men. Clearly, the report illustrates that women workers have suffered more due to the pandemic-induced lockdown than their male counterparts.

Meanwhile, as per new data released by UN Women and the United Nations Development Programme, an estimated 87 million women and girls are living in extreme poverty in India in 2020 and this number is expected to increase to around 100 million by 2021 in the wake of the Covid-19 pandemic. In fact, the pre-pandemic poverty rate for females in India was 13.3% compared to 12.1% for males. But by 2021, 14.7% of women and girls will be living in extreme poverty in India in comparison to 13.7% of men. This again shows the disproportionate economic impact of the pandemic on women.

Conclusion

Empowerment of a women is a process that leads women to claim their rights to have access to equal opportunities in economic, cultural, social and political spheres of life and realize their full potential. This progress has to be accompanied by their freedom in decision making both within and outside their home with the ability to influence the direction of social change. Women make enormous contributions to the economy, whether in business, on farms, as entrepreneurs or employees, or by doing unpaid care work at home.

Without gender equality and empowerment, the country could not be just, and social change wouldn't occur. Therefore, scholars agree that women's empowerment plays a huge role in development and is one of the significant contributions of development.

CHAPTER SEVEN

Post-Pandemic Impact on Indian Working Women

Introduction

The COVID-19 pandemic has been a major shock to our societies and economies, highlighting society's reliance on women on the front lines and at home, while also exposing structural inequalities in every sphere, from health to the economy, security to social protection. Women and girls face disproportionate impacts with far-reaching consequences in times of crisis, when resources are strained and institutional capacity is limited, which are amplified in contexts of fragility, conflict, and emergencies. Hard-won victories for women's rights are also in jeopardy. Responding to the pandemic is about more than just redressing long-standing inequalities; it's also about creating a resilient world that benefits everyone, with women at the forefront of recovery.

"It is the responsibility of women to hold the social fabric together – whether at home, in health centres and schools, or caring for the elderly – all of this is unpaid care work (and it continues to increase)," explains Mita Lonkar of the Chaitanya Foundation in New Delhi, India, one of many UN Women NGO partners in India providing critical support to women and their families as the country struggles to cope with the COVID-19 pandemic's second wave.

"Because the majority of those on the front lines of the pandemic are women, resources such as healthcare, education, and training for women are critical," Lonkar adds. "Women are especially vulnerable economically because their personal finances are weaker and their employment opportunities are limited."

Since January 2020, India has reported over 27 million cases of COVID-19 infection and over 300,000 deaths – figures that many experts believe are significantly underestimated. Hospitals are running out of beds and oxygen, medications are running out, and vaccines are in short supply as infection rates rise. Cyclone Yaas made landfall last week, causing massive looding and displacement in the country's coastal areas.

The emergency's scope is unprecedented, and as with any crisis, women and girls, particularly those from poor and marginalised communities, are among the worst affected. Women account for 34–42 percent of COVID-19 infections, according to data from at least seven states. The needs are vast, ranging from basic necessities such as food, personal protective equipment, hygiene and sanitation products, and vaccines to longer-term assistance to help women return to work and obtain start-up financing.

In India, the second wave of COVID-19 resulted in unprecedented losses. Without the means to absorb economic shocks and mitigate the health crisis, the poorest and most marginalised, including women and girls, face greater risks. They are providing for their families, maintaining their livelihoods, and leading efforts to combat climate.

UN Women and health sector experts respond to some frequently asked questions about COVID-19 and how it affects Indian women and girls.

The pandemic serves as a stark reminder of how important women are at all levels. Women are on the front lines of the COVID-19 response as health professionals, community volunteers, transportation and logistics managers, scientists, doctors, vaccine developers, and more. Women make up 70% of the health workforce worldwide, especially as nurses, midwives, and community health workers, and they also make up the majority of service staff in hospitals as cleaners, launderers, and caterers. Despite these figures, women are frequently left out of national and global decision-making on COVID-19. Furthermore, women are still paid significantly less than men.

Are women and girls at more risk of contracting COVID-19 than men?

The coronavirus has infected over 30 million people in India. COVID-19 is a virus that can infect people of all sexes and ages. Some women and girls, on the other hand, may be at greater risk because they are poorer and lack information and resources, or because they work in the health and service sectors as caregivers and workers.

In India, women account for a large percentage of all healthcare workers, including more than 80% of nurses and midwives. However, they are largely absent from decision-making roles in the health sector, and they are paid significantly less than their male counterparts. Women make up only 13%

of the COVID-19 task force at the national level.

Restrictive social norms, gender stereotypes, home quarantining, and resource diversion to combat the COVID-19 pandemic can limit women's access to health care and make them more vulnerable to health risks. Several women have been trapped at home with their perpetrators as a result of global lockdowns, and incidents and reports of violence against women have been on the rise around the world. Due to the COVID-19 emergency response and global lockdowns, women's access to sexual and reproductive health services has been severely hampered. Their mental health has been severely strained as a result of their multiple responsibilities.

How has COVID-19 impacted women's employment in India?

Supporting women's recovery from the pandemic would be a wise investment for governments and could help mitigate the long-term impact of the pandemic on future generations, a study by Dalberg suggests.

Women made up only 24% of the workforce in India before the pandemic, but they accounted for 28% of all job losses as the pandemic spread. During the lockdown, women lost nearly two-thirds of their income, and as their unpaid workload increased, they were far more likely than men to report a lack of sleep. The increased household burden could make it more difficult for women to re-enter the workforce, resulting in long-term economic consequences. The crisis has disproportionately affected historically vulnerable women, such as Muslim, migrant, and single, separated, widowed, or divorced women.

Women have been pushed out of work and into poverty as a result of wage disparities and the burden of unpaid care. Even before the pandemic, women's earned income in India was only one-fifth that of men's. During COVID-19, more women have lost jobs around the world, including in India. According to a recent report by the Center for Sustainable Employment at Azim Premji University in India, only 7% of men lost their jobs during the first lockdown in 2020, compared to 47% of women who lost their jobs and did not return to work by the end of the year. Women fared even worse in the informal sector. Between March and April of this year, 80 percent of rural Indian women working in informal jobs were employed.

Despite the hardships encountered during the research, interviews revealed many inspiring stories of women's resilience: women supporting entire villages as they navigated the health crisis, spreading awareness, and serving as community lifelines and frontline workers throughout the crisis.

Many people made difficult decisions to keep their families afloat, such as providing family meals with fewer supplies and, in some cases, going without food to ensure that their children were fed. Some people took money out of their savings to pay for things like household supplies, food, and medicine, as well as internet packages for their children's continued education, for which many people also had to provide tutoring.

Women and children from the community gathered in Batla House, Okhla, New Delhi, at a Saheli Samanvay Kendra (SSK) community centre. The Indian government has established SSK community centres across the country to serve as local incubation centres for women's self-help groups, skill training, and public health information. The SSKs work in "Anganwadi" centres, which are part of the Indian public health care system and provide basic health care to rural and marginalised populations. These centres have remained open throughout the COVID-19 pandemic, providing free meals, immunizations, and health screenings for children, pregnant and lactating mothers, and assisting women in accessing government assistance programmes. Women learn tailoring and sewing, as well as computer skills and beautician techniques, at the SSK centre in Batla House.

Socio-Economic Impact of COVID-19 on Women Migrant Workers

In India, the COVID-19 pandemic has wreaked havoc on domestic migrant workers. This brief presents the key findings from a survey of 10,161 women migrant workers from 12 Indian states to address the pandemic's gendered impact on migrant workers. Women migrant workers were found to be burdened with the dual burden of earning a living and providing unpaid care at home, according to the study. Furthermore, compared to pre-pandemic levels, their incomes dropped by more than half during the pandemic. In light of this, this brief discusses the importance of social protection measures for Indian women migrant workers in the areas of food security, cash assistance, government health insurance, and domestic violence protection.

Has COVID-19 increased violence against women in India?

Violence against women remains a major threat to global public health and women's health during emergencies, according to the WHO. Domestic violence cases have increased since the COVID-19 outbreak began, according to reports from China, the United Kingdom, the United States, and other countries. In India, the National Commission for Women has reported an increase in the number of reported cases of violence. Women's vulnerability to violence can be exacerbated by stress, disruption of social and protective networks, and a lack of access to services.

Gender-based violence is on the rise as a result of economic and social pressures, as well as movement restrictions and cramped living quarters. Prior to the pandemic, it was estimated that one in every three women would face violence at some point in their lives, a human rights violation with a USD 1.5 trillion economic cost. As overburdened healthcare systems and disrupted justice systems struggle to respond, many of these women are now trapped at home with their abusers and are at increased risk of other forms of violence. Online forms of violence against women and girls in chat rooms, gaming platforms, and other places are likely to increase as more people spend time online with movement restrictions in place. –– Women as they navigate deserted urban or rural public spaces and transportation services under lockdown, essential and informal workers –– such as doctors, nurses, and street vendors –– are at increased risk of violence. Economic effects of the pandemic are likely to increase sexual exploitation and child marriage, putting women and girls in fragile economies and refugee situations at risk. UN Secretary-General António Guterres called for an end to all forms of violence everywhere, from war zones to people's homes, in April, and for all efforts to be focused on ending the pandemic.

Domestic violence shelter and support services have been classified as "essential" by the Indian government, marking a significant step forward in the COVID-19 response. In India, 700 One-Stop-Crisis centres remained open during the first and second waves of the pandemic, assisting over 300,000 women who had been abused and required shelter, legal assistance, and medical attention.

Another positive step is the current draught of the anti-trafficking bill, which will be tabled in Parliament soon and will increase penalties for perpetrators and make reporting of such crimes mandatory.

Is the COVID-19 vaccine safe for pregnant or menstruating women?

While reports suggest that men, the elderly, and people with weakened immune systems are the most vulnerable to COVID-19, the greater caregiving role that women and girls are expected to fulfil may jeopardise their mental health and well-being.

COVID-19 vaccines have not been shown to cause harmful side effects in menstruating, pregnant, or lactating women. In addition, there is no evidence that COVID-19 vaccines cause infertility. In fact, if COVID-19 is contracted during pregnancy, there is a higher risk of severe symptoms.

The World Health Organization has also confirmed that women who are breastfeeding can safely receive the vaccine, and that no active COVID-19 disease-causing virus has been detected in breast milk. Vaccinating lactating mothers has been shown to be effective.

How can we support women and girls in India during the COVID-19 crisis?

Social workers use public awareness campaigns to ensure that women receive verified information about disease prevention and vaccination, as well as to raise public awareness about gender-based violence. Through our programmes, we are providing women with access to education and vocational training via digital and distance learning, as well as assisting them in finding employment and starting small businesses. In COVID-safe spaces, we collaborate with our national partners to provide survivors of gender-based violence with shelter, financial and legal assistance, and medical assistance.

Discussion and Recommendations

Every crisis impacts women and girls differently than men, because of existing gender norms and inequalities. To build back better and equal from the COVID-19 crisis, policy, investment and action must be shaped by women and girls and deliberately target them.

What can be done to mitigate the risk to family planning programs?

• Social marketing and FP service delivery organisations could help the government ensure a steady supply of reversible contraception and relieve some of the strain on the public health system.

• Self-care items such as condoms, oral contraceptive pills, emergency contraceptive pills, pregnancy test kits, and sanitary pads should be readily available in pharmacies. Furthermore, ensuring the continuity of the contraceptive supply chain is critical in order to avoid stock outs in districts and PHCs.

• To ensure continued access to family planning services, ASHAs and other community-based health workers should be supported.

• Family planning counselling should be available through helplines, telemedicine services, community radios, chatbots, and mobile services.

• In this time of crisis, the government should make use of partnerships with NGOs to support information and service delivery. In this time of crisis, the government has recognised the critical role of NGOs in providing services to vulnerable groups. Many women and children will need to be able to access essential non-COVID-19 healthcare services, so ensuring easy mobility and smooth operations of NGOs providing health and family planning services will be critical.

What can be done to address mental health issues stemming from the COVID-19 pandemic?

• Women's psychological support services should be integrated into primary health care.

• The creation of a comprehensive crisis prevention and intervention system that includes epidemiological monitoring, screening, referral, and targeted intervention to alleviate psychological distress.

• Public awareness campaigns to ensure that vulnerable groups, such as women, are well informed about mental health services' availability and accessibility.

• Increased research funding for mental health.

• Strengthening mental health services by establishing a cadre of trained professionals.

What can be done to address violence against women during the COVID-19 response?

• Governments and policymakers should include measures to address violence against women in COVID-19 preparedness and response plans.

• A public health response to violence against women is being developed.

• Providing survivors of violence and early detection cases with preventive, curative, and systematic referral support.

• Educating healthcare providers so that they can provide better care and counselling to victims of violence.

• Hotlines, telemedicine services, shelters, rape crisis centres, and counselling for victims of violence must all be made available.

• Greater emphasis on violence reporting in COVID-19 response plans.

Conclusion

As the worst of the pandemic fades and vaccination rates steadily rise, rebuilding India's economy and bringing the newly impoverished back into the middle class is a critical policy challenge made more complicated by the country's uniquely gendered nature and the fact that, as in most crises, women bear the brunt and have the most difficult time recovering.

Recognizing women's physical ordeals is, without a doubt, the first step toward empowering them. Too many of them are anecdotal due to a lack of academic or policy intervention to assess their statistical significance. It is also critical that the government enlists the help of existing organised corporate structures to implement compassionate labour policies, particularly from a political standpoint. a gendered perspective While recognising invisible household chores has its own set of challenges, and it's difficult to catalyse interventions in the domestic sphere, the structured and easily amendable work sectors must help India's women reclaim their lost morale. Existing skill-building programmes run by the government of India, such as the Pradhan Mantri Kaushal Vikas Yojana scheme (PMKVY), must be implemented uniformly across our urban spheres, identifying capable and determined women and cultivating in them the entrepreneurial appetite to create jobs and responsibilities as the economy recovers.

Finally, the transformation must come from within us. As women move outdoors, work must be shared responsibly by all. Stakeholders must band together to prioritise women's education and health, as well as to actualize women's empowerment through education and health.

CHAPTER EIGHT

Women Entrepreneurship In India

Introduction

Entrepreneurship is the act of starting a new company or revitalizing an existing one in order to capitalize on new opportunities. An entrepreneur is anyone who starts a company. He looks for and reacts to shift. An entrepreneur has been described in a variety of ways. Economists regard him as a fourth factor of development, alongside land labor and capital. Sociologists believe that some societies and cultures encourage entrepreneurship, such as in India, where Gujarati's and Sindhi's are known for their entrepreneurial spirit. Others believe that entrepreneurs are inventors who come up with new product, business, or methodology concepts. As a result, entrepreneurs shape the economy by generating new resources, employment and goods and services. However, according to an analysis, it's not about making profits, getting the best ideas, understanding the best sales pitch, or implementing the best marketing plan. It is, reality, a mindset toward creating something different as well as an activity that adds value to the entire social eco-system. It is the psyche makeup of a person. It is a natural state of a mind that evolves as a result of his or her surroundings and experiences, causing him or her to think about life and career in a certain way. From the beginning, entrepreneurship has been a male-dominated phenomenon, but time has changed that and brought women to the forefront as today's most unforgettable and inspiring entrepreneurs. Women entrepreneurs make up about 10% of all entrepreneurs in India, according to estimates, and the proportion is increasing year after year.

DISCUSSION:

Women entrepreneurs are characterized as individuals or groups of individuals who start, organize, and operate a company. Women entrepreneurs are described by the Indian government as an enterprise owned and operated by women, with a minimum financial interest of 51percent of the capital and at least 51percent of the employment produced in the enterprise going to women. Because of the push and pull factors that allow women to have an autonomous occupation and stand on their own two feet, women entrepreneurs are starting businesses. The driving force behind this desire is a desire to make independent decisions about their lives and careers. Women who are burdened with household duties and domestic tasks years for freedom. Women entrepreneurs choose a career as a challenge and a desire to try something different as a result of these factors. Pull factors are a term used to describe such a situation. While in push factors, women are compelled to participate in business activities by their families, and the burden of duty is thrust upon them. The basic issue that a women faces is that she is female with a weaker sex. In addition, she has a dual obligation to her family, culture, and work. Many women do not have the blessing of their elders if their joint families split up. Male concerns about a woman's position and ability still exist. Women in rural areas are often employed in low-wage, back-breaking farm work or as handicraft assistants. It is believed that imparting a skill to a girl is a waste of time because when she marries, she takes the skill with her. Women are held away from it by social attitudes in both urban and rural areas. Even the govt and licensing agencies often ask women a series of questions, doubting their ability to run a company. Women must rely on middlemen for marketing, who will eat up a large portion of their earnings. Despite of the fact that women entrepreneurs are serious about preserving quality and meeting deadlines, there is a natural inclination to doubt the quality of the products they make.

STEPS TAKEN BY GOVERNMENT

THE WOMEN ENTREPRENEUR PLATFORM (WEP): It was launched by NITI AYOG with the motive of providing an ecosystem for upcoming young women entrepreneurs across the country.

BHARATIYA MAHILA BANK: It was founded with the motive of providing financial assistance to underprivileged women who want to start their own business.

DENA SGAKTI SCHEME: The loan scheme is a solution for all women entrepreneurs who want to make out in the manufacturing and food processing sectors.

MUDRA YOGNA SCHEME: This is the one of the top schemes launched by the government of India to enthusiastic women entrepreneurs who are looking to start a small business with minimum efforts such as retails shops, beauty parlor, tuition centers or any small food outlet.

ANAPURANA SCHEME: This is the first scheme introduced by the government of India to uplift the condition of women Entrepreneurship in India way back in the year 2000. The govt of India provides women Entrepreneurs in the food, beverages and catering industry.

SHREE SHAKTI LOAN FOR WOMEN ENTREPRENEURS: This is a unique scheme run under SBI to support women entrepreneurship by providing certain concession.

All these initiatives have one thing in common: they were created with the goal of improving the status of women entrepreneurs in this country. However, putting these plans in place properly is easier said than done. The motivation behind such initiatives and schemes has always been optimistic, and if successfully implemented, they have the potential to transform India's entrepreneurial landscape.

SUGGESTIONS FOR THE GROWTH OF WOMEN ENTREPRENEURSHIP

Another important aspect of the plan should be to make it easier for women entrepreneurs to enter areas with high growth potential. To encourage women in emerging sectors, special incentives, tax rebates, duty reductions, and subsidized land and machinery can be provided. Women who work in such targeted sectors can be given special recognition and awards.

A constant effort should be made to inspire, promote, empower, and collaborate with female entrepreneurs.

Women in the community will receive vocational training that will allow them to understand the production process and management.

To help women network with other female entrepreneurs, international, national, and local trade shows, industrial exhibitions, seminar and conferences should be held. The key thrust areas for enhancing women's entrepreneurship potential through education and training are higher education incentives for women from rural areas, advanced training programs for women's management development, and the establishment of polytechnics and industrial institutes for women.

CONCLUSION:

Women's involvement in the field of entrepreneurship is growing at a significant place, so we can say that we are in a better position today. Efforts are being made in the economy to ensure that Indian women have equal opportunities in all fields, and laws guaranteeing equal rights of participation in the political process, as well as equal opportunities and rights in education and jobs, have been enacted. However, government-sponsored development activities have only benefited a small group of people, namely urban middle-class women. Nearly 45 percent of India's population is made up of women. Women's position in economic growth is also being taken to encourage women to start businesses. The resurgence of entrepreneurship is urgently needed, with a focus on educating the female population, spreading knowledge and consciousness among women, and encouraging them to shine in the enterprise sector by recognizing their strengths and important role in society, as well as the significant contribution they can make to their industry and the entire economy. Women entrepreneur must be properly molded with entrepreneurial qualities and skills in order to address changing dynamics, global business challenges, and be professional enough to maintain and aspire for excellence in the entrepreneurial arena. If every citizen works with such an attitude toward respecting women's important role in society and understanding their vital role in modern business, we can very soon estimate our chances of outperforming our own conservative and rigid thinking process, which is the most significant impediment to our country's growth. We've always believed that a smart woman can get a job everyday but that if she becomes an entrepreneur, she can a make a living for at least 10 more women. Rather than relying on wage jobs sources, highly trained, technically sound, and professionally skilled women should be encouraged to run their own businesses. Young women's untapped skills can be recognized, educated, and applied to a variety of industries to boost productivity in the manufacturing sector.

For women entrepreneurship is not a bed of roses. Women participate in a variety of economic activities to supplement their family's income; however, their participation does not relieve them of their family responsibilities. Women's work has become more difficult. and full of difficulties Let us all work to help women rediscover themselves.

Teacher as a Leader

Introduction :

An effective leader helps bring any school to the forefront. The plight of schools in India is exacerbated by the lack of qualified leaders. Effective leadership cannot always be judged by equipment or infrastructure availability, leadership has qualitative measures. The real leader is one who helps the school move forward with a vision. A leader is a person who has a cleared vision and self-motivated and committed to his work. Effective leadership fostering learning environment in school. A true leader always motivates other. Leaders are always a good administrator and manager. But all administrators are not the leader. Leaders are try to make school in a learning organization with the help of human, physical, social transformation. In this case teacher educators can make new leaders. Leaders of the present age lead the team by stepping forward from behind the scenes or Leading the team from the front depends on their personal characteristics like is she a autocratic, beurocratic or democratic leader? But in general it can be said that leaders start moving towards a goal. So in order to meet the needs in the 21st century, we need an effective leader in school level. Their personalities always attract others. They are polite but efficient. This part of educational administration is therefore very important and has become the focus of discussion at present.

What is Educational Management :

Educational management is a process of planning, organizing, directing, controlling and evaluating the activities of an organization or an institution by utilizing human and material resources to efficiently fulfill the academic goals, teaching, research and other administrative work. Now a days it is evolving as a field of study and research. Educational management mainly works on achieving institutional goal or objectives, improving the principles and whole process, optimal utilization of human resources and increasing capacity and effective human resources, create an work environment, managing conflicts and improving interpersonal relationship etc. Educational management operates in educational institutions. For success of educational management there must be needed different discipline and norms with adequate freedom. So it emphasize on

- human resources
- physical resources
- curricular and controlling curricular activities.

Educational management focuses on set of short term and long term goal, planning, problem solving, communicating, decision making of curricular and controlling curricular activities in an academic calendar, effectively allocating financial resources, maintaining school and student records etc.

Basic features of educational management :

Educational management work on activity in functional level, management plays an executive role. A group of people who are employees of the organization, is known management. Management makes decisions under the under the boundaries of the organization. Whereas, educational administration like owners, takes all the important decisions, it concern with framing policies, connected with legislative decisions, so it play role is decisive in nature.

If we look into the features of educational administration, can see it is the umbrella term, educational management is under of this. These features clearly makes difference between educational administration and management.

What is leadership in education :

For schools leaders are thus more than just good managers; they are leaders of school as "learning organizations" (Darling Hammond, Wei & Andree, 2010). They are also expected to promote inclusive school cultures (Riehl, 2000). They need to be educational visionaries, instructional leaders, supervisors of policy mandates and initiatives and even community builders (DeVita, 2010). A leader is, who has the ability of problem solving better, who takes initiatives first for work to solve a problem and who can communicate and understand better the situation and psychology, is called a leader. Many of these leadership attributes are positively related to student achievement, learning and attitudes (Cotton, 2003). Notably, leadership effects on student learning occur largely because leadership strengthen teachers' engagement in the professional community, which is turn, promotes the use of instructional practices that are associated with student achievement (Wahlstrom, Louis, Leithwood & Anderson, 2010). It is also focusing on distributed school leadership is grounded in the concept of sustainable change (Fullan, 2001). Leadership must also be sustainable for those who lead through their work activities (Donaldson, 2001).

Some insights about leadership :

According to NPE (1986) school leaders in India should evolving long term planning based on the country's development and manpower needs and focuses on decentralization of educational institutions. According to NCF (2005) the teacher work behind the scenes plan and carry out the activities. Teacher need to address different psychological and physical aspects of different schools, so that an environment could be build or construct as per the uniqueness of this schools, it means it incorporate diversity. According to RTE Act (2009) clearly stated the ratio of student teacher in an educational institution, where the instructional head act as a leader. She has the power to functioning as school. According to NEP 2020 a leader should be those person who have high academic qualification and administrative, leadership capabilities along with abilities to manage complex situations. So we have seen that, here a leader may be a assistant teacher, not only the head teacher. It proves that, the scenario is changing.

Who is the all time leaders? :

NCERT stated in their hand book on School Leadership (2014) there is a significant difference between an administrator, a manager and a leader. An efficient administrator is very disciplined in their works regularly in his educational institution. A manager wants to maintaining tasks and relationships and run his academy smoothly. But a leaders work is beyond that. Because a leader has firstly a cleared vision about their schools and they motivates others to work for his institution eg. his colleagues, parents and even his beloved students. The vision should be shared vision and they need to come out from their limitations, boundaries.

So we observed that a leader should be believe himself, confident, honest, empowered, committed, good communicator, decision maker, courage, empathetic, resistance, intelligence, transformation, empowered and creative in nature. These qualities are commonly seen in leaders.

Characteristics of leadership :

Cleared vision : An important characteristic of a leader is to have a clear idea of his vision and mission. Which will help him to move forward with his educational institution towards improvement as mentioned by NCERT in their hand book on School Leadership (2014). The nature of a leader's work and his commitment will help him to distinguish his organization from other teachers. He will be self-motivated to meet his goals and fulfill his vision, he will try to do as much as possible. Institutional growth and improvement will be the only goal of the leader in school leadership.

Motivator : In the case of school leadership, a leader cannot fulfill all the responsibilities by himself from the center of his power. He will share all the responsibilities among his other colleagues and she will make hes decision by taking opinions of the colleagues. Many teachers do not want to involve themselves in this complex decision making part without teaching. But a true leader will inspire his colleague about this and ensure that they are all members of t same family. By participating in various activities of the school, a leader can explain his true nature. If she is able to maintain a democratic environment in school, maintain the dignity of all and give equal importance to all then her colleagues will stand for her.

Dynamic Personality : In school leadership, a leader has to be a dynamic person. She is not just a teacher. She will have to co-operate with the Guardians, students, other leaders, policy makers. In addition to teaching, a school leader has to be busy with administrative work inside and outside the school. She need to address and manage the workplaces healthy relationship with colleagues. A leader must have a dynamic personality to fulfill every mission. Not all situations are under human control yet a leader can solve various problems by his personal qualities and professional skills.

Good communicator and interpreter : To solve any problem one has to reach its center. In the case of school leadership, in order for a leader to solve a problem, She must first get to the root of the problem and then interpret the problem. It is the ability of cognition and communication also. It will be easy to solve the problem whenever it is possible to build proper communication. One more thing a leader needs to be proficient at is to guess in advance future situations, means a role of predictor. This does not mean that a leader can solve all problems by guessing in advance.

Brave : A leader must be brave from her heart. Because only with a courageous mindset can face all t problems, danger and thrive to resolve this problem. Only a brave man is able to lead his team forward. And she is the brave one who can personally accept the failure of the team as her own failure. Failure will not shy away from her team's responsibilities but will motivate the team to work harder. A tendency to learn from failure can be noticed in leaders.

Deconstruction : In school leadership, a leader will always be ready for change and will always welcome change positively. Because the sign of modernity is to change oneself by maintaining the values with the present time. At present, in addition to teaching, a teacher needs to be tech savvy teacher, a leader, good administrator, knowledge provider, organizer, openminded, counsellor, facilitator for school needs. They need to reconstruct and deconstruct themselves all the time.

Self assessing question to promote leadership :

•Are the academic leaders ready to serve his work in teacher community ?

• Are the leader understand local needs or societal aspects ?

• Are the leader believes in collectiveness ?

• Are the leader practice to create democratic environment ?

• Are the leader agree to lead from the back ?

• Are the leader practice sustainable work in teaching learning ?

• Are the leader properly address students needs ?

• Are the leader ready for incorporating ICT ?

• Are the leader believes in partnership ?

• Are the leader ready to guide his students to be a future leader ?

• Are the leader practice child's holistic development approach strategies ?

• Are the leader understand the transformation ?

Role of teacher as a leader :

A]Relational trust : It is important for the head teacher and the teacher to have a little bit of trust in the relationship because if there is trust in the relationship, there will be no distance between them and Then leadership can be made more effective. Only then will they be able to trust each other with any organizational responsibilities, will there be no pressure on anyone to take responsibility for any work.

B] Conflict : Conflicts between teachers can lead to disagreements centering on a task or decision. A true leader can help them resolve this conflict and lead to better relationships.The more conflict-free the environment on the school premises, will make better understanding. In a conducive environment, everyone will be able to play their role and fulfill their responsibilities. The biggest thing is that the students will get all the benefits.

C] Positive staff culture : The more positive staff culture of the educational institution, the faster the improvement of that educational institution is possible. In this case everyone performs a certain task together and maintains and friendly environment between them. Everyone gets equal dignity equal importance so no inferiority complex can be seen in anyone. Therefore, the role of the head teacher in building a positive staff culture in the campus is undeniable.

D] Contextual aspect : Every problem has a specific perspective. A leader must judge true perspective to resolve any conflict. The importance of any problem can be realized through perspective analysis. This shows how deeply rooted a problem is or what the nature of a problem is. Being able to analyze the problem makes it easier to move forward towards its possible solution. The educational institution focuses on the learner's perspective or the organizational perspective.

E] Increase school effectiveness : To increase school effectiveness, a leader needs to focus on school-based management. Teachers motivation can make the connection between school-based management and school effectiveness. As a result, school leaders' and other school teachers can directly participate in any work and move forward towards meeting the school's goals. The direct motivation of the leader acts as a catalyst in this case.

F] Distributed leadership : Distributed Leadership makes a sense of responsibility of work among every member of the school and also helps to take responsibility. Working together takes less time and effort and less tendency to fail. There is no fear of failure, work can be done with joy because everyone works by giving their valuable assistance, feedback. Getting any work done through this collaboration and cooperation was our first learned value in ancient society.

G] Knowledge production : Needless to say, the role of knowledge in educational institutions. Knowledge production today is not limited to the acquisition of knowledge, On the contrary, it can be said that standing in the 21st century, the practical field of knowledge is of utmost importance. However, today educational institutions are creating unprecedented examples by constructing new knowledge. Gathering information through the internet is not a big deal these days. Here effective leadership can show schools a new direction by building knowledge. A leader can transform a school into a learning organization through his personal mastery.

H] Leader as a reflective practitioner : For teachers professional development reflection is an important criteria. Through this strategy they can assess themselves in the classroom. NCERT stated in their hand book on School Leadership (2014)Teacher, who practice this into their classroom daily are called reflective practitioner. In these area a teacher can evaluate his work, proficiency level. It helps teachers to interpret, improve teaching learning and lead towards leadership.

Role of a teacher as leader after lock down :

• Our education system has been most affected by the Corona virus. So after the lockdown, the education system will have to be revived by using SDG Goal 4.

Where Quality Education has been addressed.

• We need to try to bring back sustainable education through effective leadership.

• Promote sufficiently inclusive education in the educational institution so that all students can return to school. In educational institutions where leaders believe in the Inclusiveness, it will be possible to launch it more quickly.

• After lock down new needs to be identify and focus on solving them, ensure the more engagement of students and their holistic development.

• Teachers need to start working again as collaborator with the other stakeholders, organizations in the field of education.

• ICT integration, Web-based learning needs to be promoted with more importance. For this, leaders need to be prepared with special training. New pedagogy and methodology must be invented.

• In the new socio-economic system, students' entrepreneurship must be given importance by teachers. This is where the leader will help his team move forward by training from behind the scenes and Will create future generation leaders

• Another important aspect of effective leadership is emotional intelligence. With the help of emotional intelligence a leader can take care of his students, because we all know that during pandemic the students have gone through a very difficult time. Teacher also can regulate others emotion as well as his own. Through curriculum and teacher can create positive school learning climate. Through the use of emotions a teacher can promote students thinking. It helps maintain healthy relationships in workplace. Control and regulate our own emotions also helps to achieve institution goal.

Conclusion :

Now it is proved that leadership is not just a matter of inherent or inborn quality, it can be nurtured through training. It is expected that the current leaders will be multitasking. None of us have ever experienced post covid normal situation before. It's a completely different and new situation for us. Only an efficient leader can face this new situation. As a result schools need to focus on building school leadership more and this leadership can be nurtured in teacher training institutions. For example, now we see that Government of India also took initiatives for capacity building of teachers through Swayam portal online continuous professional development programme, conducted various workshops .The continuous training updated teachers in school ,college and other institutions. We heard that leaders are always passionate about their work and self motivated. So these kinds of online or face-to-face training empowering our existing teachers towards leadership. As a professional they need lead their institution.

CHAPTER TEN

Empowering Women in Times of Bloodshed

Introduction

Women's empowerment is the mechanism in which women elaborate and reinvent what they can do, be and achieve in a situation that they have been denied before. However, when talking about women's empowerment, empowerment means accepting and allowing people (women) who are on the outside of the decision-making process into it. Empowerment can be defined in many ways.

The recent Supreme Court rulings on granting women officers a permanent commission is seen as a landmark step towards women's empowerment and corrective change to avoid perceived gender bias against women. Women's role in the

The Indian army began in 1888 when, during the British Raj, the "Indian Military Nursing Service" was formed. Women were first inducted as officers into the armed forces in 1992. India's military has 1.2 million active personnel in total. Apart from military specialist forces such as the Garud Commando Force, MARCOS, Para commandos and so on, women were not allowed to serve in combat units such as cavalry, armoured corps and mechanised cavalry. But women have been inducted into different arms and branches of the three services over the years. It is added that women should not be named to top roles such as colonels or brigadiers, since most soldiers are men from rural backgrounds who are not "mentally conditioned to recognise female officers in command, so introducing women to this existing patriarchal structure can hardly be seen as" gender advancement "in 2015 without challenging the underlying principles of masculinity." There are more than 3,500 women in the military, but before the Modi government approved an Indian Air Force (IAF) programme in 2015 to introduce them into the fighter stream, front-line combat positions were off limits to them. The Army is mostly regarded as a men's preserve, but enough women have fought valiant battles to crack the myth, from Rani of Jhansi in the past to Indian Air Force Squadron Leader Minty Agarwal. Women are expected to deride their femininity and work harder than men to gain parity in the eyes of their peers in order to survive within the Army. The Ministry of Defense of India has reported that in the preceding two years, a dozen women officers in the armed forces have lodged allegations of sexual harassment and discrimination. The number is noteworthy considering the national pattern of low reporting of sexual harassment in general and the fact that in the predominantly male-dominated Indian military, women constitute a tiny minority. The presence of women in the military is therefore yet another manoeuvre to disguise the subjugation and service of women as women's emancipation. There may have been a fall in the gender barrier, but the fight against inequity is far from over.

Why is it Needed?

- **Women Empowerment:** Earlier women were not allowed in the Permanent Commission, which had created a glass ceiling. That ceiling has now been shattered with a Supreme Court ruling allowing permanent commission for women.
- **Equality of Opportunity:** Without giving the command role to women, we cannot analyze that they are not competent. It is a denial of an opportunity.
- **Changes in Nature of War:** With changes in technologies, the nature of conventional war has also changed. Consequently, issues related to Prisoners of Wars have decreased a lot. The doors must be kept open for the women, and if they are suitable on the basis of objective criteria, they should be enrolled.
- **Stronger Armed Force:** The verdict will ensure that regardless of gender, the potential of the best of India's youth will be utilized in its Armed Forces.

As they have learned this since their youth, women promote participation and share power and knowledge, and yet are ruthless when the situation demands it. Naturally, it is up to them to improve their colleagues' self-worth and get the best out of them, a rare yet very sought-after attribute in a successful leader. Our armed forces open their doors very hesitantly to women. It is important to make their position more broad-based. If we analyse the characteristics needed for a successful professional soldier and compare them to men and women in order to find out if they are equivalent or not on that standard, women may be better off facing a hue. The most significant aspect is professional integrity, which admittedly requires a certain degree of physical health. Women's liberation and autonomy and change in their political, social , economic and health status are essential goals in their own right. These are important priorities for sustainable growth, too.

ROLE OF WOMEN

There are no areas of employment in the modern world that women have not delved into. To accommodate women, terms such as chairman and cameraman have been rephrased as chairperson and cameraperson. Under the authority of the woman-her spirit and resources-many a male dominated workplace has crumbled. The Indian Armed Forces, considered a male-dominated workplace for a long time, now have brave, bold women, shaping every role and setting examples for all. Women have worked in different bodies in administrative and technological capacities, but fighting capacities for them, originally in the military police, is a new beginning. The position of fighting in the Indian Army has been an exclusive domain of men for a long time now. Finally, the latest judgment of the Supreme Court acknowledged gender equity in the Army by allowing female officers to be in command positions. It took several years for women to arrive at a point where they are now still eligible for fighting positions in the armed forces. If we analyse the characteristics needed for a successful professional soldier and compare them to men and women in order to find out if they are equivalent or not on that standard, women may be better off facing a hue. As they have learned this since their youth, women promote participation and share power and knowledge, and yet are ruthless when the situation demands it. Naturally, it is up to them to improve their colleagues' self-worth and get the best out of them, a rare yet very sought-after attribute in a successful leader. Our armed forces open their doors very hesitantly to women. A stage has come, however, when their position has to be made more broad-based.

FACILITIES PROVIDED TO WOMEN

A special screening board was set up by the Army to recruit women officers for the Permanent Commission. This follows the historic decision of the Supreme Court in February this year, empowering all female officers to seek a Permanent Commission in the Army. The PC means that they will continue to serve in the Indian Armed Forces until they withdraw. A Senior General Officer leads the screening board and includes a woman officer of the rank of Brigadier. To add fairness to the procedure, female officers have been allowed to witness the proceedings as observers. The order of the Ministry of Defense specifies the award of the Permanent Commission in 10 streams to Short Service Commissioned (SSC) Women Officers. Army Air Defence (AAD), Signals, Engineers, Army Aviation, Electronics and Mechanical Aerial Engineers (EME), Army Service Corps (ASC), Army Ordnance Corps (AOC), and Intelligence Corps are the 10 streams that have now been made available to the permanent commission of women officers. At present, the Army is offering women officers in two branches a permanent commission — Judge Advocate General (JAG) and education. Under the SSC, female officers are initially admitted for a term of 5 years, which can be extended to 14 years. Permanent commissioning would make it possible for them to work before retirement age.

EQUALITY OF SEXES

Armed forces equality is a little different because the point is not about freedom here; it is about having an obligation, an obligation to one's country. To claim that "I want equal pay and services, but you go and fight wars" does not seem morally acceptable to women in the armed forces. In February, the Supreme Court ruled that women could serve as military commanders, sweeping aside the government's position that male soldiers were not ready to follow orders as "disturbing" from female officers. In comparison to the warfare that India has encountered in the past, the Indian government should understand that the essence of warfare in the future is going to be entirely different. A strong nation such as India needs to improve its military capabilities for sustained growth by inducing more women into the military, keeping in mind the evolving domain of the battlefield. The Supreme Court also directed the government to extend permanent service to all women officers, which has only been applicable to men so far, signalling a shift towards gender equality in the predominantly male bastion. SC relies heavily on women's stereotypes and their physiological characteristics. SC concluded that as a weaker group , women are stereotypical and constitutionally deficient. Over the time , the government maintained that women are not permitted in commanding and fighting positions due to inherent physiological differences between men and women. In addition, "sex perceptions" were based on submissions such as those citing pregnancy and motherhood as reasons for not granting permanent commission to women.

The judgment upholds the right to equality in the Constitution

- A professional force does not discriminate on the basis of gender; it works because of training, norms and culture.
- The spirit of the order is the principle of non-discrimination. According to Article 16, Gender only cannot serve as the basis for inequitable and unequal treatment in any sphere, including in defence forces.
- It also held that rights to equality under Article 14 needs to be prescribed by a right to rationality that forbids any "blanket" and "absolute" prohibition.

With this women will get the same opportunities and benefits as their male colleagues, including ranks, promotions and pensions, and be allowed to serve longer tenures.

RECOMMENDATION AND FINDINGS

It is unfortunate that there are some old hats in 2020, mainly retired generals, who still believe that women in the forces have to remain the 'weaker' sex. Their claims reflect the conventional sexism toward women and point to the well-known evidence about the different heart rates and greater biceps of men and their capacity to scream even louder. Issues of women's role in fighting

Physical issues

- The natural physical differences between the sexes in height, strength, and body structure make women more susceptible to certain kinds of injuries and medical issues. During rigorous and intense training, this is particularly so.
- In most female applicants, pre-entry physical fitness levels appear to be lower compared to males, and thus, there is a higher risk of injuries among women while training requirements remain the same for both sexes.

Physiological issues

- In fighting situations, the normal processes of menstruation and pregnancy make women particularly vulnerable. Lack of sanitation and privacy can lead to an increased incidence of genitourinary infections.

- The influence on the reproductive health of women of prolonged deployment in rugged terrain and gruelling physical exercise is still uncertain.

Social and psychological issues

- Women, particularly their children, tend to be more attached to their families. This translates into greater emotional stress and the need for social support during long separations from the family to maintain them.
- Isolation is another social aspect that leads to mental stress in women in the military. This is due to the fact that men, especially in war zones, far outnumber women in the military.
- Military sexual trauma (MST) and its effect on the physical and mental well-being of female combatants is a serious concern.
- MST can lead to severe long-term psychological issues, including posttraumatic stress disorders (PTSDs), anxiety, and drug abuse.

Conventional Barriers

- Cultural obstacles in society may be the main obstacle to the induction of women in war.
- The implications of inserting a few women in an almost exclusively male preserve, in cramped quarters, in inhospitable terrain, isolated from civilization, might lift society's conservative eyebrows.
- The approval of the orders of the female officers by the jawans is another major issue to be investigated.

CONCLUSION

Women in the military have a tradition that, through various cultures and countries, spans over 4,000 years into the past. Women have played many such roles throughout history, from mediaeval warrior females to women soldiers currently serving in conflicts. A mixture of myth and exaggeration, combined with a few true accounts of unique women, is the past of women in war. The most obvious reason is the fact that women can physically be weaker. Therefore, they will not possess the physical features necessary for being fighting soldiers. Indeed, strong remarks made by the court against the government's gender prejudices come as a welcome relief. Equally, the equal effort and service they put forth is appreciated by ensuring that women will hold permanent commissions in the army. However, the Supreme Court strongly reprimanded the government for its apparent gender bias and directed it to enforce its decision within the next three months.

Most observers welcomed the decision by the top court as a decision towards "gender equality," with women now being able to get the same rights and benefits as their male counterparts, including ranks, promotions and pensions, and being allowed to serve longer tenures.

To conclude, women constitute half of the world 's population, and there is gender disparity in every nation on the globe. Whole societies are destined to perform below their capacity before women are granted the same possibilities that men are. The biggest need for an hour is a shift in women's social attitudes. Women should not be maltreated in any way, but every right should be granted to them instead.

References

- Bhat, Ahmad Rouf. (2015). Role of Education in the Empowerment of Women in India, *Journal of Education and Practice*, Vol.6, P.10.
- Bhat R.A. (2015). Role of Education in the Empowerment of Women in India, *Journal of Education and Practice*, 6(10), 188-191.
- Bhat, T. (2014). Women education in India need of the ever, *Human Rights International Research Journal,* Vol.1, P.3
- Dominic B., Jothi C.A. (2012). Education- A tool of Women Empowerment: Historical study based on Kerala society, *International Journal of Scientific and Research Publications*, 2(4), 2250-3153.
- Gandhi on Women: Collection of Mahatma Gandhi's Writings and Speeches on Women. Retrieved April 19, 2021 from https://www.azquotes.com/quote/602685
- Gandhi, M. K., Young India, p.406
- GOI: Annual Report (1996-97), Department of Education MHRD, New Delhi, 1997
- Nandela, Krishnan, Gandhi on Women's Empowerment, Retrieved April 19, 2021 from www.mkgandhi.org/articles/womens_empowerment.htm
- Nisha Nair. (2010). Women's education in India: A situational analysis, *IMJ*, 1(4), 100-114.
- Ramachandran V. (1998). Girls and women education: Policies and implementation mechanisms; case study: India. Bangkok: *UNESCO*. Principal Regional Office for Asia and the Pacific.
- Suguna. M (2011). Education and Women Empowerment in India, *International multi disciplinary research Journal*: Vol.1,Issue 8
- Suguna M. (2011). Education and Women Empowerment in India, *International Journal of Multidisciplinary Research*, VOL. 1.Issue 8.
- Speeches and Writings of Mahatma Gandhi, pp. 425, 426 ; 20-2-1918
- Rouf Ahmad Bhat,(2015)Role of Education in the Empowement of Women in India ,https://files.eric.ed.gov/fulltext/EJ1081705.pdf,
- The Times of India,(2020),https://timesofindia.indiatimes.com/topic/Women-Empowerment,2020

- Vedrana Milosevic,(2010) Women's impact on development in India,http://www.diva-portal.org/smash/get/diva2:293945/FULLTEXT01.pdf,January,2020.
- G Angala Eswari,(2019),A Study on Role of Women in Economic Development in India,http://www.shanlaxjournals.in/journals/index.php/economics/article/view/619
- Prakhar Mandhre,(2016),A REVIEW ON: ROLE OF WOMEN IN INDIAN ECONOMY,
- Rashmi Panwar, Dr. Monika Dave, Role of Women Workers in Indian Economy IJSSHR, Vol. 4, Issue 1, Month: January - March 2016
- Ejaz Ghani, William Kerr, and Stephen D. O'Connell,Promoting Women's Economic Participation in India, February 2013
- Bhasin, V. (2007). Status of tribal women in India. *Studies on Home and Community Science, 1*(1), 1-16.
- Zehol, L. (2003). Status of tribal women. *Anthropology of northeast India: A Textbook*, 293-306.
- Keya, P. (2011). Socio-economic status of tribal women: A study of a transhumant Gaddi population of Bharmour, Himachal Pradesh, India. *International Journal of Sociology and Anthropology, 3*(6), 189-198.
- Chishty, S., & Singh, N. (2018). Nutritional status of tribal women (Saharia and Meena), Baran district of Rajasthan, India. *Nutrition & Food Science.*
- Rao, K. M., Balakrishna, N., Arlappa, N., Laxmaiah, A., & Brahmam, G. N. V. (2010). Diet and nutritional status of women in India. *Journal of Human Ecology, 29*(3), 165-170.
- Dada, S., Ashworth, H. C., Bewa, M. J., & Dhatt, R. (2021). Words matter: political and gender analysis of speeches made by heads of government during the COVID-19 pandemic. *BMJ global health, 6*(1), e003910.
- Gausman, J., & Langer, A. (2020). Sex and gender disparities in the COVID-19 pandemic. *Journal of Women's Health, 29*(4), 465-466.
- Madgavkar, A., White, O., Krishnan, M., Mahajan, D., & Azcue, X. (2020). COVID-19 and gender equality: Countering the regressive effects. *McKinsey Global Institute.*
- Chatterjee, S. S., Chakrabarty, M., Banerjee, D., Grover, S., Chatterjee, S. S., & Dan, U. (2021). Stress, sleep and psychological impact in healthcare workers during the early phase of COVID-19 in India: a factor analysis. *Frontiers in Psychology, 12*, 473.
- Rao, G. S. N. G., & Mohan, R. (2016). Status of women entrepreneurship

in India. *International Journal of Multidisciplinary Education Research,* *5*(5), 2.

- Sarbapriya, R., & Ishita, A. R. (2011). Some aspects of women entrepreneurship in India.
- Rao, S. T., Rao, G. T., & Ganesh, M. S. (2011). Women entrepreneurship in India (a case study in Andhra Pradesh). *The Journal of Commerce,* *3*(3), 43.
- Deshpande, S., & Sethi, S. (2009). Women entrepreneurship in India. *International Research Journal, 2*(9), 13-17.
- Mahajan, S. (2013). Women entrepreneurship in India. *Global Journal of Management and Business Studies, 3*(10), 1143-1148.
- Goyal, M., & Parkash, J. (2011). Women entrepreneurship in India-problems and prospects. *International journal of multidisciplinary research, 1*(5), 195-207.
- Cotton, K. (2003). *Principals and students achievement : what the research says.* Association for supervision and Curriculum Development.
- Darling-Hammond, L., Wei, R.C., & Andree, A. (2010). How high-achieving countries develop great teachers. *Stanford Center for Opportunity Policy in Education.*
- DeVita, C.(2010). Four big lessons from a decade of work. In Wallace Foundation (Ed.), *Education Leadership : An agenda for school improvement,* 2-5. Washington DC : The Wallace Foundation National Conference.
- Donaldson, G.A. (2001). *Cultivating leadership in schools : Connecting people, purpose and practice.* New York : Teachers College Press.
- Fullan, M. (2001). *Leading in a culture of change.* San Francisco, CA : Jossey-Bass.
- National Curriculum Framework 2005, NCERT.

REFERENCES

www.ingramcontent.com/pod-product-compliance
Lightning Source LLC
Chambersburg PA
CBHW071358130726
47996CB00002B/978